P9-CPZ-373

Beyond Words

Beyond Words

Picture Books for Older Readers and Writers

Edited by Susan Benedict & Lenore Carlisle

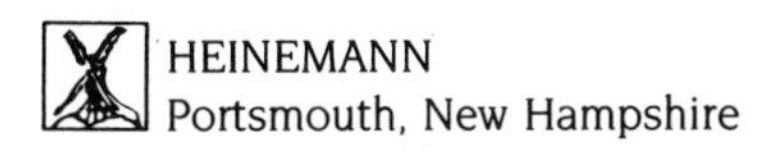

HEINEMANN
Portsmouth, New Hampshire

Heinemann Educational Books
361 Hanover Street
Portsmouth, NH 03801-3959
Offices and agents throughout the world

© 1992 by Heinemann Educational Books, Inc.
All rights reserved. No part of this book may be reproduced in any form or by electronic or mechanical means, including information storage and retrieval systems, without permission in writing from the publisher, except by a reviewer, who may quote brief passages in a review.

Every effort has been made to contact the copyright holders and students for permission to reprint borrowed material. We regret any oversights that may have occurred and would be happy to rectify them in future printings of this work.

Library of Congress Cataloging-in-Publication Data
Beyond words : picture books for older readers and writers / edited by Susan Benedict and Lenore Carlisle.
p. cm.
Includes bibliographical references.
ISBN 0–435–08710–X
1. Children—Books and reading. 2. Children's literature—Illustrations. 3. Illustrated books, Children's. 4. Picture books for children. I. Benedict, Susan. II. Carlisle, Lenore.
21037.A1B57 1992
028.5'35—dc20 92-11964
CIP

Front-cover photo by Kas Schlots-Wilson.
Design by Jenny Jensen Greenleaf.
Printed in the United States of America.
92 93 94 95 96 9 8 7 6 5 4 3 2 1

028.535
B573

Contents

Contributors

Susan Benedict is a fifth-grade teacher at Moharimet School in Madbury, NH. She has a doctorate in reading and writing from the University of Massachusetts. She teaches graduate courses in composition process at the University of Southern Maine, where she is a lecturer. Her publications include chapters in *Breaking Ground* (edited by Hansen, Newkirk, and Graves, Heinemann, 1985) and *Alternative Perspectives in Assessing Children's Language and Literacy* (edited by Bloome, Holland, and Solsken, Ablex, in press).

Rudine Sims Bishop is Professor of Education at The Ohio State University, where she teaches courses in children's literature in a graduate teacher education program. She is active in the National Council of Teachers of English and the International Reading Association. Currently editing an annotated booklist of multicultural literature, Rudine is the author of *Shadow and Substance* and *Presenting Walter Dean Myers*.

Phyllis Brazee is Associate Professor of Reading and Language Arts at the University of Maine, Orono, Maine. She teaches in an integrated, team-taught undergraduate methods block and also teaches graduate courses in literacy. In addition, for three summers she has directed an institute on integrating the curriculum in the elementary school for teams of teachers and principals. Finally, she co-directs with Dr. Brenda Powers the summer Reading/Writing program for graduate students and local children. This experience is based on the concept of the integrated curriculum.

Lenore Reilly Carlisle is a Language Arts Resource Teacher at Fort River Elementary School in Amherst, Massachusetts. She has also taught preschool, ninth-grade English, ESL and college courses. She has a master's degree in children's literature and a doctorate in reading/writing from the University of Massachusetts.

Ruth Tietjen Councell is an artist living in western Massachussetts. She has worked as an illustrator and designer for the University of California at Riverside and as a freelance illustrator. Her picture books include *Country Bear's Good Neighbor* and *Country Bear's Surprise* by Larry Brimner, and *Handel and the Famous Sword Swallower of Halle* by Bryna Stevens, a CBC/IRA Children's Choice for 1990.

Tricia Crockett, an honors student, is in her junior year at Oyster River High School in Durham, New Hampshire. She plans to work toward a baccalaureate degree following high school graduation. Pieces of her writing have been published in *Merlyn's Pen*, April/May 1991 ("Benediction"); *Workshop 2: Beyond the Basal*, 1990; and *Seeking Diversity, Language Arts with Adolescents*, 1992.

Georgia Heard is a poet and teacher who travels widely throughout North America talking with teachers and students about writing. She is the author of a new poetry–picture book for children entitled *Creatures of Earth, Sea, and Sky: Animal Poems* (Boyds Mills Press, 1992) as well as a book on teaching poetry, *For the Good of the Earth and Sun* (Heinemann, 1989).

Janet Hickman is Associate Professor of Education at The Ohio State University. She teaches courses in children's literature and has published several novels for young people, including *Valley of the Shadow* and *Thunder Pup*. She is co-author of *Children's Literature in the Elementary School* and former editor of the children's book review column for *Language Arts*.

Carolyn K. Jenks reviews books for *School Library Journal* and *Horn Book* publications. She has been a children's librarian for many years in public and elementary school libraries. She has taught children's literature at the university level, been on the Newbery Award Committee of the American Library Association, and continues to work on projects that help to further high quality in children's literature.

Bijou Le Tord was born in Saint Raphael, on the French Riviera. She has written and illustrated more than fifteen books for children, including *The Deep Blue Sea* and *The Little Shepherd*. She is well known throughout the U.S. as a writer, storyteller, photographer, and lecturer. Ms. Le Tord is a member of the Society of Children's Book Writers as well as the founder and regional chairperson of the Society's East End Long Island Chapter. She is also a member of the Authors' Guild. She teaches "The Art of Picture Book Making," a workshop she designed specifically for teachers and librarians. Ms. Le Tord lives in Sag Harbor, New York.

David E. Ludlam is working on a doctorate in reading and writing at the University of Massachusetts, Amherst. He teaches English at Smith Vocational High School in Northampton, MA. He has published and presented nationally on his research interest of peer-group writing instruction.

Thomas Newkirk is a Professor of English at the University of New Hampshire. He directs the New Hampshire Writing Program, a summer institute for teachers, which attracts participants from across the country. He is the editor or co-editor of several books, including *Understanding Writing: Ways of Observing, Learning, and Teaching* (with Nancie Atwell) and *Breaking Ground: Teachers Relate Reading and Writing in the Elementary School* (with Don Graves and Jane Hansen). He is the author of *More Than Stories: The Range of Children's Writing*, and he has recently finished *Listening In: Children Talk About Books (and Other Things)*.

Linda Rief is a full-time seventh- and eighth-grade language arts teacher at Oyster River Middle School in Durham, NH. She is also an instructor in the University of New Hampshire Summer Reading and Writing Program. Her first book, *Seeking Diversity: Language Arts with Adolescents* was recently published by Heinemann. She is also the author of articles in *Learning*, *Language Arts*, and *Educational Leadership* and chapters in *Breaking Ground* (edited by Hansen, Newkirk, & Graves), *Workshop* I, and *Workshop* II (edited by Nancie Atwell).

Barbara Bagge Rynerson currently teaches a combination first- and second-grade class in Durham, NH. She acts as a consultant to other teachers who are interested in learning more about literature-based reading programs and the teaching of writing. She has a master's degree in reading and writing from the University of Massachusetts, Amherst. She is the author of " 'This Fish Is So Strange to Me': The Use of the Science Journal" in the forthcoming *Workshop* IV (edited by Thomas Newkirk) from Heinemann.

Sara R. Weidhaas is an honors student in her junior year at Oyster River High School in Durham, New Hampshire. Her artwork has been featured on the cover of the middle school yearbook and the high school handbook. She was awarded first place in the seacoast region D.A.R.E. poster contest, and her artwork has been displayed in student and youth art shows at the University of New Hampshire and in Portsmouth, NH. She will be attending college upon completion of her secondary education.

Preface

Susan Benedict

When I moved from teaching primary to teaching intermediate grades, I brought my picture books with me; this was the children's literature I knew and loved. However, I didn't immediately take these books out of the closet; that didn't happen for three years. I continued to haunt book stores for new picture books, but these books were for me, not my students. For lack of other storage places I began placing some of my favorite picture books on the bottom shelves of my classroom bookcases.

As I struggled to demonstrate writing to my students, using the novels they were reading for support, it became abundantly clear that I was not going to write a novel and most of my students weren't either. I began to use my favorite picture books for writing demonstrations: Cynthia Rylant's *The Relatives Came*, Nancy Willard's *Nightgown of the Sullen Moon*, Peter Parnall's *Winter Barn*, Jane Yolen's *Sleeping Ugly*.

Later, I discovered my students reveled in and profited from reading picture books as well: Lauren read and reread lines from Ann Turner's *Dakota Dugout*; Beth's eyes softened as she read Mem Fox's *Wilfred Gordon MacDonald Partridge*; B.J. began reading *Wreck of the Zephyr* and then read every other Van Allsburg book in the library; Vera B. Williams' *String Bean's Trip to the Shining Sea* was a backwards trip across the country for Nathan who had just traveled it from West to East; Bobby went on repeated pig hunts trying to discover all the hidden pigs in his repeated readings of Anthony Browne's *Piggy Book*; Jarrod and Jeff laughed over the Stupids, characters they had not visited in a long time. When these books were placed beside the chapter books in my classroom, a door was reopened for my students, and the seed for this book was planted.

Between the covers of this volume the voices of learners, some of whom are also teachers, will speak to you about how picture books have invited them to go beyond words. Rudine Sims Bishop and Janet Hickman frame the book. They know a reader is never too old to enjoy a good picture book. Enjoyment, they say, is one of the primary reasons anyone—young or old—should read a picture book. Tom Newkirk picks up that thread when he explores "the problem with pleasure." He and Barbara Rynerson allow us to eavesdrop on good talk about books with children younger than eight. We have come to delight in the freedom of expression and discovery with young children, yet we're still surprised by the deep connections young children make. These voices are included in this volume to underscore this good talk and to remind us of the importance of keeping it alive with older students. Lenore Carlisle shows that good talk about picture books can and does continue to flourish with upper-elementary students. Her students read and respond to picture books, and their discussion enables and encourages them to explore philosophical questions.

In my chapter, my students demonstrate how picture book authors and illustrators have been their silent writing partners. Linda Rief says that picture books are ~~even~~ especially for middle school students. Because Linda values these authors, her students do too. Linda's students Tricia Crockett and Sara Weidhaas chronicle their own personal journeys with picture books. Sara shows how a study of an illustrator encouraged her to integrate her science learning and her art. Tricia's journey with picture books led her unexpectedly to a benediction. David Ludlam shows that picture books have brought his high school students to new levels of literacy.

Carolyn Jenks has a broad definition of picture books. Within the boundaries of her definition she provides a rich description of picture books that are cataloged within and beyond the confines of easy fiction in her library. Phyllis Brazee reminds us what learning is and, through picture books helps us to rediscover asking Why? Why? Why?

Georgia Heard points out how often good picture books border on poetry. Good picture books frequently convey meaning through the same qualities poetry does. Bijou Le Tord, Ruth Councell, and Ann Turner give us insiders' views of the making of picture books. They each show us how the bits and pieces of their lives and their research are nurtured into texts and illustrations, which make picture books an art form all their own.

These essays, then, are an invitation for you to place picture books along side those weightier volumes on your book shelves. An invitation to open the covers for yourself and your students and step inside—to read, talk, explore, play, and write. Picture books belong not only in the warm circle of bedtime reading, nor just in the hands of primary children and teachers; they belong in any classroom where students don't sit on tiny chairs and on any night stand where the reading light goes on after eight.

Beyond Words

1

Four or Fourteen or Forty: Picture Books Are for Everyone

Rudine Sims Bishop and Janet Hickman

The students lean forward in their seats, all eyes on the reader and the book. As the reader holds up the pictures, or walks around the room holding the pages toward them, they shift around in their chairs to get a better view. When the reader lowers her voice to a near whisper, they strain to hear every word. As they listen, they respond—sometimes with a thoughtful silence, sometimes even with tears. The book is thirty-two pages long, and its text is so brief it can be read in its entirety in about ten minutes. Most of the space in the book is taken up by pictures, which provide their own narration of the story, both illuminating and expanding on the text. The students are being introduced to Eve Bunting's *Fly Away Home*, illustrated by Ronald Himler. It is the story of a homeless father and son who have taken up residence in an airport. The listeners are moved by the story and are eager to hold the book and examine it closely on their own. This sort of experience is a familiar one, a part of the class routine, and they look forward to it as one of the best parts of the day.

Elementary school? First grade, perhaps? No, this is a university class. The listeners are adult students earning advanced degrees in education. The books they listen to and examine with such rapt attention are most often picture books, selections from a genre many assume was left behind with kindergarten and the bedtime story. The experience of sharing picture books in class brings home the point of this chapter and this volume: good picture books can be enjoyed by people of all ages.

The course in which we read picture books aloud is not a course in picture books, but a survey of children's literature. Frequently, it is organized around genres: fiction, nonfiction, realism, fantasy, poetry, traditional literature, biography and, of course, picture books. One of the assumptions underlying our classes and all our work with children's literature is that it is itself real literature, worthy of study, differing from other literature only in its adaptations to an implied primary audience of young, less experienced readers.

What is a Picture Book?

Usually we begin the course with the picture book and, as we do here, with definitions. Surprisingly, experts do not always agree on the definition of a picture book. For purists, a picture book is a picture storybook, a fiction book with a dual narrative, in which both the pictures and the text work interdependently to tell a story. It is a tale told in two media, the integration of visual and verbal art. Where the pictures are complimentary but not necessary for constructing story meaning, purists might refer to the work as an illustrated book rather than a picture storybook.

One example of a fine picture storybook that can be enjoyed across a wide age range is Uri Shulevitz's retelling of an Eastern European Hasidic parable, *The Treasure*. It begins, "There once was a man and his name was Isaac." It goes on to tell how Isaac, who was terribly poor, was directed in a dream to go to the capital city to search for a treasure. He obeys, only to discover that the treasure is actually back home. The tightly woven text is elegant in its simplicity. Shulevitz has chosen his words carefully, not one is superfluous. Many pages contain just one or two lines of text; others have no text at all. The pictures delineate the setting, the physical characteristics of Isaac, all the detail and specificity not contained in the text. Furthermore, the pictures are carefully wrought artistically and thoughtfully arranged to make the reading of the book a visually aesthetic experience. The pictures and text are a perfect blend, supplementing and enriching each other, but each depending on the other to make the book whole and greater than the sum of its parts.

A book that is clearly an illustrated book as opposed to a picture storybook—and here we stretch the point to make the point—is Barbara Cohen's selection and adaptation of Chaucer's *Canterbury Tales*, with illustrations by Trina Schart Hyman. Here words stand alone, and the pictures, relatively few in number, act to underscore what the print says about setting, character, and action. The pictures have value as artistic achievements in their own right. They also serve to clarify the text, especially for readers who are unfamiliar with the medieval period. Nevertheless, the pictures could be removed without in any way diminishing the tales; this is an illustrated book, not a picture storybook.

For many authorities, and for most practical purposes, *picture books* include any book that appears in picture book format. Such books have in common a number of characteristics: they are usually thirty-two pages long, although they may be as short as twenty-four and as long as forty-eight pages; pictures appear on every page or double page spread, with the pictures taking up most of the space; text is relatively brief. Just about any definition of a picture book, however, includes the requirement that, in the marriage of words and pictures, the two partners share the responsibility of making the book work.

Using this broader definition, picture books for all ages can include books from all genres of children's literature, as well as some subgenres unique to picture books. For example, alphabet books are, by their very nature, always picture books. We tend to assume that the purpose of such books is to help young children learn their ABCs by associating the names of familiar objects with their initial letter. Some alphabet books, however, are clearly intended for an older audience. Somewhat in dictionary fashion, they use the alphabet as an organizing structure to provide information about a particular topic. An example is the 1977 Caldecott Medal winner *Ashanti to Zulu* written by Margaret Musgrove and illustrated by Leo and Diane Dillon. It introduces information about twenty-six African tribal groups, one beginning with each letter of the alphabet. Although the text on each page is generally limited to one paragraph, it is well beyond the brief labels typical of alphabet books for young children. The Dillons' softly colored illustrations were carefully researched and designed to provide information about the people of each group, their typical manner of dress, their homes, and their natural surroundings.

In recent years, there has been a trend toward publishing more books with briefer texts. This has meant that some types of books that have been considered—in part because of their length—suitable for an older audience, are being produced in relatively brief picture book format. Diane Stanley, for example, has produced picture biographies such as *Peter the Great* and *Shaka, King of the Zulus*, which was illustrated by Stanley and co-written by her husband Peter Vennema. Her mother, Fay Stanley, wrote the text for *The Last Princess: The Story of Princess Ka'iulani of Hawai'i*. These biographies are nearly forty pages long, and they usually contain a great deal more text than do picture storybooks. However, the full color paintings, which appear on every doublespread, enrich and extend the text by offering a kind of "photo album" of the subjects' lives, as well as a clear depiction of the geographical settings and the historical times in which they lived.

More and more frequently, writers and writer/artists who create other kinds of nonfiction are also using the picture book format to reach a wider audience. Leonard Everett Fisher, for instance, has produced a number of informative and artistic books about world landmarks. *The Tower of London* and *The Great Wall of China*, illustrated in black and white acrylics, describe these structures and place them in the context of their history.

As with many good nonfiction picture books, the art in these books invites readers not only to absorb information, but to engage in critical interpretations of the events depicted.

Poetry is often assumed to hold its own images, but a number of relatively long poems have recently been presented as the text of picture books. Robert W. Service's well-loved poem *The Cremation of Sam McGee* has been made into a picture book with paintings by Ted Harrison. The introductions by Pierre Burton and Harrison provide biographical and other information that give some insight into the creation of the poem and the book. They also offer an explanation of Harrison's choice of bright colors to depict a landscape usually drawn in blues and whites to reflect the cold climate. This artistic choice demonstrates the potential of poems presented in picture book format to offer new perspectives on familiar texts.

Even though the scope of picture books is wide and becoming wider, many of the picture books best remembered by older students and adults are fictional. Picture books that tell realistic stories are still abundant today, as are fantasy stories and folktales, and other traditional literature. Many variations of well-known tales such as *Cinderella* and *Little Red Riding Hood* are readily available, illustrated by numerous artists using a wide variety of artistic media.

In fact, if there is one striking thing about children's books in the 1990s it is how many of them are published in a picture book format. Visually satisfying books of every sort dominate the children's book market. One recent survey showed that almost two-thirds of the children's books purchased in bookstores were picture books of one kind or another. Publishers usually print many more copies of a new picture book title than of a novel, anticipating large sales. A quick look at publishers' catalogs also shows that books with plentiful pictures claim much of the space on new lists for each season.

Why Picture Books?

One explanation for the remarkable popularity of picture books is that we have come to see new value in them. Traditionally, adults have offered picture books to young children to amuse them and to introduce new concepts or knowledge about the world. These are still good reasons. Now, however, large numbers of teachers and parents also recognize what an important role picture books can play in young children's language growth and their development as readers and writers. As other contributors to this volume ably demonstrate, picture books can serve older children and adolescents in much the same ways.

One of our tasks here is to describe the value of picture books for older readers. As with younger children, the place to begin is enjoyment. Picture books are a source of personal pleasure and aesthetic satisfaction for all ages. One of the books that make upper-grade readers laugh is Jon Scieszka's *The True Story of the Three Pigs by A. Wolf*; they feel that they are in on the joke during the wolf's clever explanation of his behavior, and they seem to delight in Lane Smith's dark, exaggerated visualization of the action. Older readers also find gratification in stories that reflect their experiences and concerns. Personal issues that are crucial to middle graders are often explored in picture books based on myth. The theme of *The Story of Jumping Mouse* by John Steptoe touches children who may sense a connection between their own efforts to grow up and the quest of the mouse, whose painful sacrifices transform him into a creature of unexpected glory. The dramatic black-and-white illustrations, with their surprising close-up views and unusual rendering of sunlight, provide added appeal for the older reader.

The pleasures of a book like Richard Lewis's *All of You Was Singing* are largely aesthetic. The author's retelling of an Aztec myth about the origin of music offers cadenced, lyrical prose interpreted in evocative, carefully designed illustrations by Ed Young. The real value of this book is that it is beautiful. Its artistry speaks most clearly to readers who are patient and reflective, those who have had considerable experience with stories, poems, and pictures. Students might want to respond in some way, but it is enough simply to let such a book work its own quiet magic.

We also value picture books, fiction and nonfiction alike, for what they can teach us through their content. Many picture books offer readers the past, like *My Place* by Nadia Wheatley and Donna Rawlins, which peels away the history of an Australian city neighborhood decade by decade, or Arielle Olson's *The Lighthouse Keeper's Daughter*, illustrated by Elaine Wentworth, the story of a courageous nineteenth-century girl on the coast of Maine. The experiences of many cultural groups appear in picture books, although these titles are still relatively few in number. *Tar Beach* by Faith Ringgold provides a glimpse of an African American family in Harlem just before World War II. The black tar rooftop of their apartment building is their vacation spot on hot summer nights, as well as the launching pad for Cassie's fantasies about flying and vanquishing the racial discrimination that keeps her father out of a trade union and on a fruitless search for work commensurate with his skills. Science finds its way into picture books, too, sometimes explicitly as a book's topic, sometimes as part of the background for a fictional story. Such a combination of imagination and carefully researched information occurs in *The Last Dinosaur* by Jim Murphy, illustrated by Mark Alan Weatherby.

It may be too obvious to say that picture books teach with pictures as well as words, but it is a critical point. Try to imagine what the content of Aliki's *The King's Day* would be without its detailed drawings of the architectures and trappings of daily life that surrounded Louis XIV. Or consider Ken Robbins' description of an amaryllis in *A Flower Grows* without the artful, hand-tinted photographs that show every stage of growth from bulb to flower and back.

The educational values of picture books, however, go beyond their content. Hearing and reading picture books, thinking about and working with them, can help children become better readers and writers. This process is easy to see in primary classrooms, as children revisit favorite storybooks, making the words and the form their own. Picture books can also furnish strong support for older readers as they continue in their literacy development.

For example, picture books can help readers build greater awareness of language. A case in point is *Kites Sail High* by Ruth Heller, which calls deliberate attention to language. The topic is words—verbs, to be exact. Boldly designed illustrations of high intensity color keep interest from waning as the rhymed text defines the technical vocabulary of tense, mood, and voice. Usually books provide a more subtle form of instruction in effective ways of using language; they teach by example. George Ella Lyon's *Come a Tide*, illustrated by Stephen Gammell, demonstrates how much just a few words of well-chosen dialogue can do to suggest characterization: When Mama offers the neighbors a ride in the family truck to escape rising flood waters, one replies, "Joe won't go till he finds his teeth so I've put a pot of coffee on." Memorable imagery and vivid language are exemplified again and again in the picture book stories of Jane Yolen and Byrd Baylor, to name just two of many other authors who are fine stylists.

Picture books also offer opportunities to explore and learn the conventions by which illustrations communicate meaning. Being able to read pictures as well as print is increasingly important in our society, and picture books provide one natural vehicle for developing this facility. Most children, or at least those who have been read to, come to school knowing some of the basic conventions of illustrations, but the finer points of how pictures work remain for older children to discover. In Ed Young's *Lon Po Po: A Red-Riding Hood Story from China*, for instance, we notice that the really striking feature of the mostly red and black cover is the wolf's staring white eyes. This is not just because the eyes are blank but because light, bright accents have dominance over a darker background. Several illustrations show how the position and relative size of objects in a picture affect our interpretation of it. One doublespread shows the wolf's shadow and the three frightened little girls, who were expecting their grandmother. The shadow's huge size in relation to the children and its position above them heightens the effect of the threat. Since what goes up can come down, an object overhead is always dangerous. Other illustrations demonstrate how the relationship of figure to ground can provide a double meaning. In one picture children might see the girls sharing their bed with the imposter wolf, or, in the alternate perspective, already in his gaping mouth.

Another value of picture books for the older reader and writer is the opportunity they present for examining form and structure. Paying attention to the way picture books are put together may help readers see story patterns that are useful in interpreting longer texts. Student writers may discover ways of organizing information or of presenting imaginative ideas that will have a marked effect on their own reports or stories. Certainly picture books suggest to children that they might use some combination of words and pictures to share information or to tell their own stories.

14

As models, picture books suggest both conventional and innovative forms. ABC and counting books, for instance, provide clear and straightforward organizational forms that still leave room for many creative elements. Examples of innovative structures are also abundant. The four *Magic Schoolbus* books written by Joanna Cole and illustrated by Bruce Degen take a playful approach to science topics. Each of the titles combines a conventional, single-narrator story with a subtext of comments by other characters in speech balloons and sidebars of pertinent information embedded in the illustrations as students' hand-lettered science reports. Mitsumasa Anno frequently presents his stories in fresh and challenging forms. His *Anno's Aesop: A Book of Fables by Aesop and Mr. Fox* is a book within a book. The illustrations for the familiar tales at the top of the page serve as inspiration for a completely different set of stories at the bottom as told by Mr. Fox, who obviously could not read the original. David Macaulay may have proved for all time that picture books are not necessarily simple with his Caldecott award-winning *Black and White*. Four separate but intersecting stories are pictured, in different styles, in four different quadrants of each double spread.

It is the great variety of ways in which authors and illustrators offer their work that makes picture books such a valuable resource. That same variety, of course, means that careful choices have to be made.

Choosing Good Picture Books for Older Readers

Learning to select good quality picture books requires learning to pay attention to both the text and the pictures and the ways the two work together. As with any literature, there can be no checklist that can be objectively applied to every book, and different readers and critics will produce different appraisals of the same book. There are, however, guidelines that can be useful for teachers and parents faced with the task of choosing from among the hundreds of picture books produced every year.

The quality of a picture book is greatly dependent on the quality of its art. Although taste in art is to a great extent an individual matter, it is possible to make judgements about how well the art for any good book seems to work. In addition to considering whether the art is aesthetically pleasing or satisfying, it is advisable to consider how well the artist has used elements of his or her craft to produce the desired effect. Bright or dark colors, heavy or light lines, round or angular shapes, opaque or transparent media—all these and more contribute to the mood, the tone, the overall effectiveness of the visual art. Examining the books illustrated by an artist such as Marcia Brown, who varies her media and her style to suit the text, could reveal how different texts seem to require, or at least benefit from, different artistic treatments.

Another criterion to keep in mind is that the quality of the text ought to match the quality of the pictures. Many current picture books contain lavish full color illustrations but do not come close to matching the visual art with literary artistry. If picture books are to serve as models of effective language use, then their texts must be well written. The brevity of picture books dictates that the text must often be concise, conveying a good deal of meaning with a few well-chosen words, imaginatively used. We have already pointed out the skill with which writers such as George Ella Lyon, Jane Yolen, and Byrd Baylor successfully use understatement, dialogue, imagery, and vivid language to create literary texts. Writers often make effective use of structural patterns as well, often resulting in books that are particularly enjoyable when read aloud. Cynthia Rylant uses repetition and an episodic structure in *When I Was Young in the Mountains*, illustrated by Diane Goode. The book recalls her life as a young child growing up in her grandparents' home in the Appalachians. Rylant stacks one warm family memory atop another, each beginning with the title phrase, "When I was young in the mountains."

Rylant's book meets another criterion of good quality picture storybooks: the pictures and the text work together to produce a harmonious whole. Each enriches and complements the other. In the case of *When I Was Young in the Mountains*, Goode uses warm browns and very soft greens and blue-grays to reflect the earthiness of the experiences and the warm relationships within the family. As in any good picture book, the choice of artist's medium, the colors used, the artist's style, even the placement of the words and pictures on the page, and the use of white space complement the text and reflect the mood and tone of the story. Even in picture books other than picture storybooks, the pictures and the text must seem as if they were made for each other, not forced into an unhappy relationship.

Literary and artistic quality are criteria that apply to picture books for all ages. The standards for books particularly suited to older readers will differ from those for younger readers in degree rather than in kind. In general, they will vary along three dimensions: content, length or complexity, and sophistication.

The content of some picture books makes them appropriate only for readers beyond the primary grades. For example, the horrible effect of war on families and individuals is the topic of several books in picture book format. Sheila Hamanaka's *The Journey: Japanese Americans, Racism, and Renewal*, based on her twenty-five foot mural, graphically tells the story of the Japanese Americans who were imprisoned in U.S. internment camps during World War II. Roberto Innocenti's *Rose Blanche* vividly shows the horrors of the Holocaust through the eyes of a young school girl who is moved to try to alleviate the suffering of some Jewish children in a World War II concentration camp.

Many other picture books, including poetry and biography in picture book format, are suitable for upper-grade classrooms because their content is related to the course of study or the interests of the students in the class. Many fine picture books are available on topics in science or social studies. Often such books can add depth to the study of a topic by providing detailed information not available in textbooks, or they can introduce a topic that is to be explored in greater depth over a longer period.

Longer picture books and those that contain a great deal of text are typically considered appropriate for older readers. Such books call for an audience with the ability to sustain attention longer than most primary children find reasonable. One example is *The Mouse Couple*, a Hopi folktale retold by Ekkehart Malotki and illustrated by Michael Lacapa, a fifty-six page book. Although a few of the pages are double page picture spreads with no text, and all of the pages include illustrations, most of the pages contain between two hundred and two-hundred-fifty words. Clearly this is a folktale to be enjoyed by upper-grade students.

Length is often taken as a potential indication of complexity; the more words, the more likely a complex text. It should be noted, however, that even though longer texts seem to assume an older audience, fewer words do not necessarily exclude that audience. Some very complex stories have been told with no words at all. David Weisner's *Free Fall*, for example, relates a complicated dream sequence involving logical impossibilities, in which ordinary objects are transformed, and the boy dreamer travels through time and space, sometimes having frightening adventures. *Anno's Journey* by Mitsumasa Anno follows a lone traveler on a seemingly simple trip through a European countryside. Along the way the reader can spot numerous surprises, such as paintings by European masters and characters from folk tales, that potentially make each reader's journey unique.

As a general—and perhaps obvious—rule of thumb, the more complex and sophisticated the book, the more suitable for an older audience. Such books assume a certain amount of prior experience with complex texts and with the world in general. Anthony Browne's *Piggybook* provides pointed social commentary about the disparity between a working mother's duties and those of her husband and sons. Although young children laugh at the "piggy" pictures, older students who have met a wide range of attitudes on this issue can make richer meanings from Browne's work. Complexity is a major feature in Nancy Ekholm Burkert's beautifully crafted *Valentine & Orson*, which is based on a medieval French romance about the fortunes of twin brothers separated at birth. The story is retold in verse that echoes the period of origin, while the illustrations show the action performed as a folk play on a makeshift outdoor stage. Readers here must follow surprising twists and turns of plot, keep track of multiple layers of history and geography, plus factor in the poetic and dramatic forms—not a small task but a very rewarding one.

If books are sometimes wordwise, so are readers. The same sophistication that allows older readers to tackle more complex books also contributes to their enjoyment of some books that seem to be suited for a younger audience. *Ruby*, a retelling of the Little Red Riding Hood story by Michael Emberly, is such a picture book. It can be enjoyed as a story about a mouse who, with the help of her grandmother's friend, outsmarts a slick and dangerous cat. But readers who already know the Red Riding Hood story will appreciate, among other things, Ruby's red cape, and the book she is absorbed in (Little Red Riding Hood), as well as the twist on the traditional story. Those who know Boston, where the story is set, will find further amusement in the pictures, as will anyone who has ever tried to park a car on a crowded city street.

One aspect of sophistication is tone. In *Ruby*, the tone is humorous, making it suitable for a wide range of readers. On the other hand, *To Hell With Dying* by Alice Walker, illustrated by Catherine Deeter, carries at times a nostalgic tone, making it appropriate for older readers who can appreciate the sense of yearning for a childhood long gone.

In sum, the criteria for selecting books for older readers are relative, a matter of degree rather than kind. Basically, picture books do what any good books do. Books entertain, bringing personal satisfactions. Books teach. They teach about content, about the world they represent. They also teach about form, about literature and language, and the ways stories can be told. Because picture books present themselves in two modes, pictures and print, the possibilities are expanded and intensified. These potentials exist whether the audience for picture books is four, or fourteen, or forty.

In this chapter we have tried to define the picture book, to explain its values to older readers, and to present useful guidelines for selecting picture books for sharing with readers beyond the age of eight. The students in our classrooms are generally much closer to forty than to four or even fourteen. What we have learned from working with them and from their responses to picture books is what we have tried, in essence, to pass on here: good picture books are dual works of art, worthy of study, capable of both entertaining and teaching, and, like all good works of art, offer something of value to people of all ages.

2

Reasoning Around Picture Books

Thomas Newkirk

A friend of mine once called second grade "the adolescence of elementary school." Second graders seem transformed—poised, socially aware, concerned about dressing right, and anxious for those signs (e.g., pierced ears) of miniature adulthood. Their drawings are suddenly conventional; faces are flesh color and not the vivid greens or blues that a first grader might choose. Friendship groups are more stable and often cliquish. And, as they gain fluency in their reading, they want to read chapter books, just as adult readers do. In the case of my older daughter, it was Laura Ingalls Wilder who displaced the picture books. With great reluctance my wife and I put aside Viola Swamp, the Wild Things, and the Stupids (whom we'd come to love).

No great harm was done. My daughter remains an avid reader. But this rapid abandonment of picture books, this tendency to think of them as inappropriate for fluent readers, is consistent with deeply rooted cultural assumptions about literacy, writing, art, and, what I have called elsewhere "the problem of pleasure" (Newkirk, 1991). It's useful to ask why we must make the case for picture books at all. What are we arguing against? Why must we argue that picture books are literature and not simply literature for young children? The answer, I feel, lies in these core assumptions.

What Is Serious Literacy?

We can start with the Western bias in favor of elaboration and explicitness, a bias that contrasts dramatically with the emphasis on suggestion and economy in Asian writing (and art). The haiku is one well-known example of Japanese poetry, and while we introduce students to haiku in schools, I suspect that many Westerners, myself included, find them unsatisfyingly brief and stark. We expect something more in the lyric tradition in which the writer's reaction to nature is more fully worked out. The haiku does not offer us *enough*.

This suggestiveness is also a feature of Chinese prose. Recently a graduate student from mainland China showed me translations of prize winning essays from college students in her country. These essays often consisted of a series of very brief vignettes, often of no more than seventy-five words, placed in a series, and separated by a row of asterisks. To the Western reader these vignettes seem undeveloped; we would expect a greater density of detail, and we would expect transitions between the vignettes. According to this student, her U.S. teachers expect almost limitless development; to do well in her writing she must "go on and on."

We can see this bias toward length even in the names we give to different types of narratives. A story of ten to twenty pages is a "short story." Presumably a story of the proper length is a novel. And that is how fiction writers often measure themselves. In my own department there are wonderful "short story" writers who think themselves failures because they have never climbed the real mountain, the novel. To be a writer one must learn to write at length. By extension, to be a reader one must learn to read at length.

The second bias favors print literacy almost to the exclusion of the visual. To read is to read print. Proponents of print literacy often see the visual as a threat. They see themselves as one of the few remaining guardians of reason and reflection in a media culture awash in images. Children are seduced by the attractions of the visual. Video games corrupt children because they supply such immediate visual gratification. In schools we can hear teachers complaining about students who *still* want to draw when they should be writing. We focus on the written message and may ignore the picture that was far more central to the students.

The problem, according to this view, is that images are open to effortless perception and enjoyment. They are visceral, unfiltered by judgement. By contrast, the reader's mind must activate the print; the reader constructs the images and concepts called up by written language. There is a deliberate transformation that is under rational control.

Underlying this preoccupation with print literacy, I believe, is a third bias—a bias against pleasure. Pleasure, after all, has been suspect since the Puritan times. Early reading instruction in the *New England Primer* was not designed to initiate children to the pleasures of reading; rather it was used for religious instruction. Without the capacity to read the Bible, one's soul was in danger. This Puritanism, in various guises, has persisted in reading instruction, and one aspect of this Puritanism is the work ethic. Learning to read should be a serious and effortful form of self-improvement, one which instills in students the capacity for self-discipline and delayed gratification. Children very early learn to see reading as work, and the language of the classroom—*work* books, *work* sheets, *work* habits—invokes the ethic of industrious application. When children are working well, they are *on task*. By contrast pleasure reading, if it exists at all, comes at the margins of the reading *work*.

If learning to read is, as I've suggested, a serious and effortful form of self-improvement, it stands to reason that children need to be properly challenged. Longer books require the student to sustain the effort of reading, to begin a job and stick with it. A third grader who reads *Alice in Wonderland* demonstrates a purposefulness that is not shown by a classmate who reads and rereads *The Polar Express*. Because picture books seem so immediately gratifying, particularly to fairly proficient readers, it follows that these books do not teach children to suspend their need for gratification. They don't require work. And, to be fair, my disappointment with Sarah's switch to Laura Ingalls Wilder was mixed with pride that she could sustain her interest in one author. It seemed . . . well, adult.

The Case for Picture Books

The case for picture books involves both what I will call a bold argument and a more modest pragmatic argument. The bold argument asserts that we need to consider picture books as literature—not children's literature—but as *literature*. And to make this case we need to take more of an Asian aesthetic perspective, one that values economy and suggestiveness over explicitness. From this perspective we can see the brevity of text not as a concession to young readers but as part of the consummate skill of writers. In addition, this bolder argument calls for a new view of *text*, one in which pictures and written language work together. Finally, this argument will challenge mechanical models of curriculum that treat texts as products to be consumed at points in the elementary grades. Once consumed, once mastered, once the *task* is done, it is inefficient and unnecessary to reconsume, remaster, redo it. But good books cannot be depleted in this way. They offer something different to readers of different ages.

It is also possible to argue, more modestly, that there are good pragmatic reasons for not packing picture books away after second grade. Even if children shift their reading to longer chapter books, their writing does not expand in this exponential way (although it too may begin to take the form of chapters). The texts children write are more likely to resemble the texts of picture books than longer books composed of extended chapters. Whatever their reading preferences they will need the picture books as models for their writing.

It is also possible to underestimate the potential of picture books for eliciting thoughtful discussion and speculation. Complexity, after all, is not simply (or even primarily) a mechanical matter of word length and clause length, numbers that can be fed into readability formulas. The possibility for discussion arises when there are *gaps* in the text, indeterminacies that a reader must resolve. No text, after all is fully explicit, and if such a text existed we would get no pleasure in reading it—there would be nothing left to do.

In the remainder of this chapter I would like to examine excerpts from discussions of picture books. They focus on the questions of plausibility and show how proficient readers uncover the complexity of books that, at first glance, might seem too simple for them. These discussions are part of a first-second grade reading program where, for thirty to forty minutes each day a group of four students meets to discuss the books they have read. The groups are chosen by a student and regularly include both first- and second-grade readers; the books shared in one session might range from picture books with no words to longer chapter books by Beverly Cleary or Patricia Reilly Giff.

What Would You Wish For

The following discussion is about Chris Van Allsburg's *The Polar Express* which Jimmy, a proficient second-grade reader, shares with the group. He begins with a summary and reads a portion of the book. As he comes to the picture where the elves are assembled to watch Santa give the first gift of Christmas, Phillip, an enthusiastic first grader, interrupts:

Phillip: Wow. That would be awesome to see that much elves. [Jimmy continues reading. Mentions "first gift of Christmas."] What would I like for Christmas—every boy's toy in the world that I don't got.

After Jimmy finishes the book, he asks for questions and comments, and there is a short discussion of other Chris Van Allsburg books. But Phillip is still interested in "the first gift of Christmas." Significantly, when adults read this book, they focus on the bell that Santa cuts for the narrator and the significance of still being able to hear it as an adult. For Phillip, and I would guess other children, the central interest comes earlier, when the boy could choose anything for the first gift of Christmas—it is as if the narrator blew his opportunity by asking for a bell. At any rate, Phillip comes back to his question:

Phillip: What would you want for Christmas if you were that boy?
Jimmy: I'm not sure.
Phillip: Do you got Nintendo?
Jimmy: No.
Phillip: If you wanted you could ask for that.

Jimmy: Anyway, this story is supposed to take place many years ago.
Pat (the teacher): Why do you say that?
Jimmy: Well, because at the end of the book it says [he reads], "At one time most of my friends could hear but as the years passed it went silent for them. Even Sarah said on Christmas that she could no longer hear its sweet sound. Though I've grown old, the bell still rings for me as it does to all who truly believe."
Pat: I don't think I ever noticed about that part at the end. It does make it so that it's a story that happened years ago.
Jimmy: And there's no such thing as Nintendo all those years ago.
Pat: No, that's true.
Phillip: I think there was no such thing as TV.
Jen: There was no such thing as electricity.

The discussion then shifts to this issue of electricity. They notice that there are no lights on the Christmas tree and they try to determine if that is because they were turned off—or because Jen was right about electricity. Then the discussion shifts to toys, and Phillip comes back to the wonderful opportunity that the boy in the story has been given.

Phillip: I know what I would want if I was that boy.
Jimmy: What?
Phillip: A New Kids on the Block tape.
Jimmy: Hmmm. New Kids on the Block I don't think were even born then.
Phillip: I think they were maybe five or six years old then.
Caren: Then why would they be singing Phillip?
Jimmy: They'd be as old as he would.
Phillip: Maybe little babies.

Jimmy seems to juxtapose at least three time schemes in his responses to Phillip. First, there is the time that the story is told, by an older man looking back at his childhood. Second, there is the time the story occurs, thirty or forty years before the time of the telling. And then there is nonstory time, the chronology of events occurring in the *real* world outside the story. Phillip wants to see the boy in the story as a contemporary, as someone in his own position who could wish for Nintendo or a New Kids on the Block tape. Jimmy, on the other hand, realizes that such a wish would violate the story time in which the events occur much earlier. If story time is matched up to *real time*, he knows that Phillip's wish is unrealistic.

If You Were an Ant

The second book discussion is about another Chris Van Allsburg book. *Two Bad Ants* shows the adventure of two ants in a kitchen from the ants' point of view. The discussion was wide-ranging, but it generally revolved around the most terrifying of the ants' adventures—the time they crawled into a toaster. Alex began by telling of a dream he had.

> Well, when they got electric shocks well last night I had a dream about this lady. She picked up the phone and then electricity started coming out into her ear and she went "Ahhhh!" and the phone was sucking her ear and she kept on screaming and her body got all wrinkled and she fell down dead.

His story drew a chorus of "ooohs" and set the stage for electricity stories from the other members of the class. Andy, for example, told about his mother's adventures:

Andy: One time my mom took a knife and stuck the tip of the knife into an electricity hole but the handle was made of wood.
Pat: And it didn't go through the wood?
Andy: No, electricity only goes through metal.
Pat: I thought it would go from metal into wood.
Andy: Yeah, but it didn't shock her because she [pause] it . . .
Pat: It was lucky.
Andy: Yeah.

This kind of parallel story telling is common in discussion groups. The shared book calls up the students' stories and these stories lead in any number of directions—in this case to issues of the conduction of electricity. It is as if the book represents a conversational turn that enables Alex and Andy to take their turns.

Just as they move from the story world to their own, they also move into the story world, as Phillip did with *The Polar Express*. First graders often see no need to act differently in this story world (Phillip wanted his Nintendo), but other readers like Jimmy and, in the excerpt below, Megan, complicate this entry. Pat begins this segment by mentioning the concept of point of view:

Pat: [*Two Bad Ants*] isn't that spooky. It's just different. Everything is from the ants' point of view so everything looks huge.
Helen: Yeah.
Andy: But I would have recognized those two holes.
Pat (laughs): You would have recognized them? You wouldn't have gone in them, especially if you were wet.
Andy: Well, if I was human and there was two big lightening holes from a giant, I would not go in there. Especially if it had a plug.
Helen: I wouldn't either.

Pat: But you know about electricity.
Andy: The ants wouldn't.
Pat: They never had any reason to use electricity.
Megan: If you got turned into an ant then you probably would know. But if you were an ant and you had never been a person, then you probably wouldn't know that it was electricity.
Alex: Yeah, it would be an ant hole.
Pat: You wouldn't know what electricity could do.

Just as in the excerpt on time in *The Polar Express*, this exchange shows Megan and Alex juxtaposing two perspectives, that of humans who know how dangerous electricity is, and the perspective of the ants. They can begin to appreciate that the characters in stories are not exactly like them. The ant cannot see the danger they see; the boy in *The Polar Express* cannot wish for what they would choose.

Is It Real?

Children also use picture books to test their understanding of physical and social worlds. Could the events in this story really happen? Do people really act this way? How realistic is this story? The sophistication of second graders, their pre-adolescent adolescence, derives from a more realistic (and in some ways conventional) view of causation. They look upon their younger siblings' beliefs in Tooth Fairies and the Easter Bunny (beliefs they had held a year earlier) as impossibly primitive. Their carefully outlined, proportional, flesh colored faces are, in their eyes, clear improvements over the more flamboyant work of first graders that we adults might prefer. The concern is for realism.

Fiction, with its mixture of the real and imaginary, becomes a testing ground for this world knowledge. These tests can be simple physical ones, such as occurred in a discussion on *Arthur's Tooth*. Earlier in the reading of the book, when Francine, Arthur's usual tormentor, had her tooth fall out onto her desk. Jimmy says, "She would be bleeding then." And Brian, a first grader, says, "Yeah, I think I know. Maybe she had the tooth already out and pretended it came out at school." This would solve the problem of blood and also not be out of character for Francine.

They return to the subject of blood later when Francine, who had been calling Arthur a baby, accidentally knocks out his loose tooth.

Jimmy: He's not a baby anymore.
Alex: He lost a tooth.
Jimmy: She knocked out Arthur's tooth.
Brian: She went poooom and Arthur's tooth went. . . .

Alex finishes reading.

Brian: He would be bleeding.
Pat: Hmmmm.
Jimmy: He would be bleeding.

The discussion then stays on the subject of blood for several minutes as each of the group members, veterans of many lost teeth, tell about how much or how little they bled, testing the events of the story against their own experiences.

Because they clearly understand the lines that divide the possible and the impossible, some of the readers in Pat's class would play with these boundaries. In the following discussion of Ezra Jack Keats' book, *The Trip*, the group talks about making a shoebox city just as Louie does in the story:

Pat: You could build any kind of scene inside.
Megan: You don't have to do buildings and a plane.
Jimmy: You can do rivers, oceans, railroad stations, anything, except for the Empire State Building in real life.
Megan: You could do the Empire State Building but it wouldn't be as tall as it really is.
Jimmy: Yeah and fit into a shoebox. [Everybody laughs.]
Caren: It would be an ant Empire State Building there.
Vicky: The shoebox would fit into it.
Caren: Yeah. The shoebox would fit in the Empire State Building.

Clearly Vicky and Caren found the exchanges between Megan and Jimmy intriguing—and Jimmy's remark about fitting the Empire State Building into the shoebox hysterically funny. The reason, I believe, is the way Jimmy and Megan are playing with the relationship of the real to the imagined, the Empire State Building as it really is and the fictionalized, miniaturized version that could go in a shoe box. The exchange is much funnier for the participants than it is for adults because it is making fun of an unrealistic world view that the participants—who now understand *real life*—have recently left behind.

This reality testing also occurs when it comes to analyzing motives of characters in picture books. The following discussion of *The Teacher from the Black Lagoon* is a good example of possibilities of interpretation that occur in a deceptively complex picture book. In it a young boy is attending school for the first day, and he has heard that his teacher, Mrs. Green, is "a real monster." He sits in his empty classroom and soon Mrs. Green comes in—and she is a *real* monster. She illustrates fractions by biting a student in half. The talk focuses on the reality of these monster scenes, and, typically, Jimmy begins with "Do you think that could really happen in the real world?" And Adam, the boy who had read the book, says, "Unh uh." A couple of exchanges later Donald comes back to this question.

Donald: Well, I don't think that this happened. I think it was a dream.
Adam: I don't think so. Because it's the first day of school and I don't think he would be dreaming in school, on the first day of school.
Pat: Well, how do you think the story goes then? You don't think he was dreaming?
Adam: No.
Pat: How do you think all those ideas came to him about those teachers?
Andy: I don't know.
Pat: Who was telling him about those teachers. How did he find out?
Adam: I don't know. Well, at the picture I was drawing [students in the class draw a picture from the book as part of their preparation for group discussion] he's looking at a paper that tells all the teachers and what they have.
Pat: So he's the first one in the classroom.
Adam: Yeah.
Pat: All by himself.
Adam: Now I think he's dreaming.
Pat: What makes you think so?
Adam: Because he's closing his eyes.
Jimmy: And he dreams about all terrible things.

It is interesting why Adam resists Donald's suggestion that the monster incidents are part of a dream. To Adam it seemed implausible that a kindergartner or first grader, nervous about the teacher he would have, would fall asleep in class before school even began. Adam wouldn't act that way, and he had difficulty imagining the boy would.

In all these excerpts we see children manipulating what Ann Dyson calls their "multiple worlds" (1989); they constantly move between the empirical world (*real life*) and the worlds rendered in the picture books. They project themselves into stories; they match story time with historical time; they use fictional stories as prompts or conversational turns that enable them to tell their own stories; and they use their knowledge of social behavior and physical causation to test the realism of fiction. This and more.

None of these acts are particular to picture books, but picture books seem to have major advantages, even (or maybe especially) for children who no longer find them difficult to decode. Their brevity allows for a sharing of the whole, for a completed aesthetic experience such as we get in the story telling around the family table. The economy of written language, the mix of picture and text, leaves much unsaid and open.

In *The Polar Express*, the boy who receives the sleighbell on Christmas morning shakes it for his parents, but they cannot hear the ringing. Even his sister, Sarah, as she gets older, loses the capacity to hear this bell. Only the boy, now a man, and others who have not lost touch with childhood can still hear. Does a similar deafness (or blindness) occur in our approach to picture books? When do we cease to hear the ringing? Why do we cease to hear the ringing?

WORKS CITED

Dyson, Ann Haas. 1989. *The Multiple Worlds of Child Writers*. New York: Teachers College.

Newkirk, Thomas. 1991. "The Middle Class and the Problem of Pleasure." In Nancie Atwell (Ed.), *Workshop* III. Portsmouth, NH: Heinemann.

3

"Whoa! Nigel, You're a Wild Thing!"

Barbara Bagge Rynerson

After sharing Maurice Sendak's *Where the Wild Things Are* with the members of her literature discussion group, seven-year-old Rachel calls on children who have questions or comments.

Ted: My favorite part is when they roared their terrible roars. But when it said at the end . . . [Turns to the end of the book.] I don't think they could sail in and out of weeks, and it [the soup] would still be hot.
Doug: He was just imagining.
Tripp: It was just imagination.
Nigel: How long do you think he was imagining?
Rachel: Probably while his mom made the supper, like maybe an hour.
Nigel: I like when he says to his mother, "I'll eat you up!"
Rachel: What would your mother do, if you said that?
Doug: I'd probably get sent to bed without my supper.
Nigel: Not me! I say things like that to my mother all the time.
Ted: Whoa! Nigel you're a wild thing!
All: Laughter.

This lively discussion is one of many that occurr during genre study of fantasy in my multi-aged, first- and second-grade classroom. During this study, the children read on their own and listen as I read a variety of picture books from this genre. The children then respond to the literature through dramatic play, art projects, both small- and large-group discussion, and writing. Although this chapter focuses on one genre study, this particular study is typical of the way in which we usually respond to and discuss literature. This chapter will focus primarily on the oral responses the children make during the whole-class discussions at read-aloud time and the conversations that develop during our literature discussion circles. The responses, which occur in these contexts, reveal the important role that the picture book plays for us as we jointly enter the authors' fantasy worlds and look at these worlds within the context of our own lives.

Genre Study and Literature Discussion Circles

As in most primary classrooms, I read picture books to my students daily. Students occasionally bring in a favorite book that they would like me to read to the class, and students often request that I read a particular book from the classroom collection. But, for the most part, I generally select the titles for our read-aloud time. I find that organizing books for read-aloud either by author, genre, or theme helps to set the stage for an in-depth study. Our follow-up discussions allow us to more easily make connections among various titles and so we are able to gain a better understanding of a set of literary works.

Beyond the read-aloud time the students have daily opportunities to read titles of their own choosing. Once a week the students meet in small groups we call *literature discussion circles* to share and discuss the titles they read on their own. Each child brings a book that he or she has recently read and enjoyed to his or her group meeting. The children take turns sharing the books with their group members. They summarize the story, tell about a favorite part, and call on classmates who have comments or questions about the story. During the question and comment time animated discussions often take place—sometimes leading group members toward a deeper connection with or understanding of the text.

During read-aloud I usually get the discussion started by asking the first question. I don't ask the children literal comprehension questions that require them to recall specific information from the text. Instead I try to get things started by asking open-ended questions that encourage them to explore the story on a deeper level. Once the dialogue starts, I help facilitate the discussion by encouraging the children to reflect on one another's responses.

During literature discussion groups, I am usually a participant in one group. I am still able to gain a sense of what occurs in the other groups by listening to tape recordings that I make of each groups' sessions. As a participant I resist any urge I may feel to lead the group. I try to let the group members feel their own way through the discussion. However, I am also sure that by participating once a month in each group the children benefit from hearing the types of questions I ask and the comments I make after a student shares a book. I also serve as a model by reflecting upon the students' thoughts and commenting on them.

Exploring Fantasy

Fantasy is a rich genre. It provides us with the opportunity to dream new dreams, enter new worlds, and explore other ways of life. Fantasy also gives us greater insight into our own reality and enables us to look at our own lives from a new perspective. Although there are many wonderful chapter books written in this genre, given the age of my students I decided to restrict our study to picture books. These are shorter to read and so leave time for lengthier discussion. I also feel that many of my students are able to read these books on their own and so have access to them beyond the read-aloud time. In many of the beautifully illustrated fantasy books, the reader needs to use both the illustrations and the text to discover the authors' messages. This is an aspect of the genre that fascinates the students. The books that I choose to study are written by such marvelous author/illustrators as Maurice Sendak, Chris Van Allsburg, Mercer Mayer, John Burningham, and William Joyce.

In choosing the literature, I look for stories that are believable within the context of the fantasy. In *The Wreck of the Zephyr*, Van Allsburg's rich illustrations and his old but wise narrator make even the most cynical reader believe that a boat could fly. I also look for a rich marriage of pictures and text. Without the illustrations, the reader would never know about the wild adventures that Shirley experiences in Burningham's book, *Come Away From the Water, Shirley*. I choose books that explore issues and themes to which my students would relate. Children are wildly entertained by the way in which a small boy confronts his nightmare in Mercer Mayer's *There's a Nightmare in My Closet*. They hold their breath in anticipation as the short-tempered teacher, Miss Potts, in Val Willis's tale *The Secret in the Matchbox*, continues to ignore the fact that her classroom is being taken over by a dragon. The stories I select take both my students and me out of our classroom and lead us into fantasy worlds where anything is possible.

When I analyze the tapes of both read-aloud discussions and the literature discussion groups, I find such a wide range of responses that I can easily group them into at least fifteen different categories of response. For purposes of discussion I have grouped them more loosely under four different headings: Reality or Fantasy, Exploring the Fantasy World, A Closer Look at Illustrations, and Delving into the Author's Message.

Reality or Fantasy

Just as the distinction between fiction and nonfiction can be blurred, the distinction between reality and fantasy can be even more confusing. Chris Van Allsburg, writer and illustrator of picture books, discusses the notion of believability when asked in an interview if he believed in Santa Claus. He replied, "I believed in Santa Claus hook, line, and sinker. I would like kids to believe the magic of *Polar Express* is a reality. . . . It's not just the gifts. It's that someone arrives at your house, walks on your roof, eats the cookies you put out. There's evidence that he's been there." Discussions about whether or not something could happen in real life are commonplace during our studies. The students engage in heated debates; everyone wants an opportunity to contribute his or her own piece of "evidence." As our discussions continue, the line between fantasy and reality becomes fuzzier for all of us.

Conversations such as the following one, which took place after we read John Burningham's *Where's Julius?* are typical. This story is about a little boy who is on a wild adventure in another part of the world each time his parents prepare a meal. His parents calmly and dutifully deliver his meals to such far away places as the Changa Benang mountains near Tibet and the Lombo Bombo River in Central Africa.

Ms. R.: Would you describe this story as fantasy or realistic fiction?

Jan: Fantasy. Well . . . no—not really. I think it's realistic fiction. I think he's just imagining. But it's fantasy if you think he [Julius] really went on those trips.

Ms. R.: So it's realistic fiction if the boy and his parents are just pretending that he takes these trips. But if he really is having these adventures, you would call this a fantasy?

Jan: Yeah.

Ms. R.: Other people say that this is fantasy. Why do you say that, Bob?

Bob: Ooh, I forgot.

Josh: He couldn't really do all those things. He could dig a hole but not all the way to the other side of the world.

Amy: He couldn't climb the mountain all in one night.

Kara: I climbed up Mount Chocorua in one day.

Josh: It depends on what kind of mountain it is.

Paul: If he started early in the morning and hiked all day, he could have made it.

Ms. R.: He could have made it?

Paul: Yeah.

Kara: You can climb up a mountain. But you can't dig a hole to the other side of the world.

Paul: Well you can but. . . .

Brian: It's impossible. It's too hot in the middle.

Paul: Well, you can but . . . you'd get burned to a crisp in the core because the core is where all the lava is and that's where all that stuff comes from. It comes out of the volcanoes. But it comes from the core. If you had an x-ray, a really high-powered one, you could take an x-ray, and you could look into the earth, and you could see all this lava and you would see it's very hot.

Ms. R.: Brian, did you want to say something?
Brian: Yeah. He couldn't get from Africa to South America in that amount of time.
Paul: Didn't you ever hear of a jet. They go super, SUPER fast!
Josh: But you can't just jump from scene to scene to scene to scene—like I can't just go, "I think I'll just go WAAAA!" And I'll be there. And then you can't just go, "I think I'll climb up these mountains. AAAAAAAAH!" I mean you can't just go, "YEEHA! I think I'll ride the rapids." And then you're on a raft. You just can't.
Anne: You can in your imagination.

Our discussions about what is real and what is fantasy brought into play our knowledge of the world, our personal experience, and in the case of Paul and Anne, the limits of our imagination.

The illustrating style of the author often plays an important role in our debates about reality and fantasy. Chris Van Allsburg's illustrations are quite realistic. His style convinces many young readers that his stories are true. After reading *The Wreck of the Zephyr*, Lynne and Christopher decide that the story is real.

Ms. R.: What makes you think that this is a true story, Christopher?
Christopher: Well, you see, it's the pictures. They look so real that it just makes me feel that it's real.
Lynne: I think the same as Christopher. The pictures look so real, that I think they are just photographs. I think he really went to this place and he took pictures of what he saw.
Christopher: Yeah! Maybe they're photographs.

The Wreck of the Zephyr is a favorite book in our classroom. Perhaps there is an aspect of the young boy's adventure that appeals so much to Christopher's and Lynne's imaginations that when the adventure is combined with Van Allsburg's realistic illustrations, these two are able to stretch the limits of their own imaginations and turn the impossible into reality.

Exploring the Fantasy World

In many fantasy books the reader is transported to worlds quite different from his or her own. The children like to talk about these fantasy worlds. Their responses show an interest in these faraway places. Christopher's comments offer a good example of this type of response. Christopher talks about the island where boats sail through the air in Van Allsburg's *The Wreck of the Zephyr*.

Christopher: I would really like to go there because if there were any bullies bothering me, I would sail up into the air and throw things down on them.

The children are often intrigued with the way many books in this genre start out as realistic fiction and then move into fantasy. A favorite activity during read-aloud time involves listening for the moment when the first fantastic event occurs. The children make a game of this by raising their hands up as soon as the story becomes a fantasy. The race is often on to see who could get his or her hand up first. Soon our discussions lead us to the observation that many of these stories move back to reality in the end. Their interest during one study prompted me to create a chart on which we could record how each story we read led from reality into fantasy and then back to reality again (see Figure 3–1). When our study was over, we looked back over our chart and the following discussion ensued:

Ms. R.: What have you learned about fantasy stories by making this chart?
Jan: It seems like the characters always go on a trip, like to the land of the wild things and the island where the boats fly, and then they go back again to where they started.
Kara: Yeah! And like the character Felix, he goes out of the painting and then when he gets out of jail, he goes back in it.
Ms. R.: Those are good observations. Does anyone want to add to what Kara and Jan have said?
Jack: In that book, *In the Attic*, the kid who was bored takes a trip up to the attic.
Tripp: That's not a very long trip.
Jack: Well it's still a trip.
Ms. R.: O.K. What else do you notice? Someone who hasn't shared yet.
Anne: Well, it seems sort of like they [the books] always start and end in the same place.
Jack: And they also sort of end just like they started. Like in *The Secret in the Matchbox*, it starts and ends the same.
Ms. R.: Is everything always back to normal when the stories end? Think about the story *Where the Wild Things Are*. Is everything the same when Max returns?
Jack: Yeah, the soup's still hot!
Sharon: Yeah. But the soup wasn't there when he left. Remember she sent him to bed without his supper. Besides how do you know that it's soup.
Jack: Because it's in a bowl silly.
Ms. R.: O.K. His supper is there when he returns. Does anyone else want to comment on the story. How have things changed when Max returns?

FIGURE 3–1: *Reality/Fantasy Chart*

Josh: Well his mother's not mad anymore. Or else, why did she bring him his supper? And Max isn't being wild anymore.

Josh makes an important observation. He notes an element crucial to this genre. In most fantasy stories the main character enters a fantasy world or experiences something fantastic. This experience usually changes the character in a significant way. When the character comes back to reality, things are never the same. The character has usually grown emotionally. The trip that Jan refers to often involves a rite of passage. Sendak refers to this experience when he talks about Max in *In The Night Kitchen*. He refers to Max as a character who is

> going through a very critical moment. . . . It is a moment that every kid goes through by him or herself. You have to. Every life has that. And you have to make a decision based on whatever logic or whatever experience you have at that moment. In Max's case he has a temper tantrum and his mother gets back at him; because she's only a human being, she gets mad right back. He has to figure out how to deal with that situation. He goes away to where the wild things are. (Trumpet Club, 1988)

Joshua is beginning to recognize these "critical moments."

When our study was over, three boys developed a strong interest in writing their own fantasy stories. They particularly loved writing *Jumanji* sequels. One day the three of them got together and made this list of suggestions for other fantasy writers in the class to use:

How to make your story a fantasy:

1. You could have your main character open something like a box or a door.
2. It might happen when your character falls asleep. They could have a dream.
3. Your character could go into another part of the house, like the basement or the attic.
4. Your character might be on a trip. A path might take them into another world.
5. Your character might get hurt. He could get a bump on the head and have a dream. He might wake up in a different place.
6. Your characters could be playing with a magic toy. The toy might become real.
7. Someone in your story might tell a story. The story might become real.

8. Your character could go inside a painting or a toy, like a dollhouse or a sand castle. Inside it would be another world.
9. Your character could fall out of something, like a window or a boat.

By Doug, Tripp, and Will

A Closer Look At Illustrations

As I stated earlier, all of the fantasy stories that I read to the children are picture books. The children respond to the illustrations in a variety of ways. Since I encourage the children to use a variety of techniques to illustrate their own stories, many of their comments relate to the authors' techniques. The children like to guess which technique an illustrator had used before I read the story. We often search through the text to see if the illustrating technique is mentioned anywhere in the book.

The children often compare the illustrations in one book to those in other stories we have read. For example, after reading *The Secret in the Matchbox*, Sarah makes the following connection.

Sarah: Those pictures remind me of *A Chair for My Mother* [Vera B. Williams].
Ms. R.: Why is that, Sarah?
Sarah: Well just look at the illustrations [Sarah pulls a copy of *A Chair for My Mother* off of a nearby bookshelf.] See how they both have borders on every page.

The children observe details in the illustrations that I had failed to notice after numerous readings. Their comments about *Where the Wild Things Are* serve as a good example of the attention they pay to details.

I was reading this class favorite for perhaps the third or fourth time. When I reached the second page, Tripp suddenly jumped up and grabbed the book from me.

Tripp: Wow! Look what's on this page. See! [He points to a drawing of a wild thing hanging on the wall of Max's house.] It says by Max.
Various children call out, "Let me see!" and begin to grab the book.
Ms. R.: Tripp, why don't you hold the book up so that everyone can see. Why do think Sendak put that drawing in the illustration? Doug?
Doug: Maybe he just liked the wild things a lot and wanted to put them in all the pictures.
Anson: Are they in all the other pictures?
Tripp: Let me see. [Tripp begins to pour through the pictures.] No. They're not on every page.

Ms. R.: Amy, what are you thinking?
Amy: Maybe he was giving us a clue.
Ms. R.: A clue?
Tripp: Like maybe he wants to give us a hint about what happens next.
Amy: Yeah. So we know he might get in trouble.
Tripp: Maybe he wants us to think that the book will be scary.

Amy and Tripp are beginning to understand the technique of foreshadowing. They both realize that Sendak has deliberately chosen to give the reader an early glimpse of a wild thing and are able to infer possible reasons for this decision.

Tripp's observations may encourage others to take a closer look at the pictures. At the end of this read-aloud session, Andrea announced that she wanted to show me something.

Andrea: Look. [She began to slowly turn the pages of the book.] First the pictures are small and there's lots of white space. Then the pictures get bigger. And now look . . . they get smaller again.
Paul: Look at the page where the wild things are. It [the illustration] takes up both pages.
Andrea: And then on the last page there's no picture—just words.
Ms. R.: Why do you think Sendak used the space that way, Andrea?
Andrea: Maybe he liked to draw wild things best.
Paul: Maybe he just got tired at the end.
Tripp: I know. The wild things are big, so he needed more room to draw 'em.
Jack: It's the wild part of the book, so the pictures get wilder.
Ms. R.: So you think that the pictures match the mood or feeling of the story. I notice that the larger pictures are also darker. That seems to help create a more exciting feeling, too.

The children are beginning to realize that illustrations play a strong role in establishing the mood or feeling that an author is trying to evoke.

In many fantasy picture books the illustrations are crucial to our understanding of the text. As the children become more familiar with this genre, their ability to find meaning in the illustrations becomes keener. An example of this occurred during a literature discussion circle. Doug shared a story entitled *The Incredible Painting of Felix Clousseau*, by Jon Agee, with his discussion group. This story, which takes place in Paris, is about a painter who creates paintings that come to life. In the beginning of the story he is hailed as a genius at the king's art contest and is awarded a medal. But when his paintings of a boa constrictor, a volcano, and a waterfall also come to life, he is thrown in jail and all of his paintings (with the exception of one of a mad dog) are destroyed. This painting saves the day when a thief tries to steal the queen's crown. The dog attacks the thief and Felix becomes a hero again. At the end of the story Felix walks into one of his paintings. After Doug shared the story with his group Tripp took the book and pointed to the last page.

Tripp: At the end, when he goes into the picture and he is going down the street in his painting, well that street looks the same as in the beginning when he was going to enter the contest. It looks just the same.
Doug: Yeah. It does. So I think he is in his painting in this one (pointing to the first illustration).
Tom: Oh, yeah! It does! He's walking out of the painting!
Rachel: It's like he leaves the painting to see what the world is like. But then he goes back.
Tom: Yeah. Because that way he doesn't have to go to jail again.

Without the subtlety of the illustrations these young readers would never discover the deeper level of meaning in this story. In the books that we read the illustrations help to bring new insights into the story. My students, with the inquisitiveness of detectives, uncover these deeper meanings and delight in their discoveries.

Delving Into the Author's Message

In many of our read-aloud and literature-circle discussions, the students and I begin to explore the notion of theme. The literature discussion highlighted at the beginning of this chapter moves into the notion of theme.

Tripp: If I were Max, I would of stayed with the wild things, 'coz then I could be the king.
Rachel: Not me! I'd go home.
Ms. R.: How about the rest of you, what would you do?
Ted: I'd go home.
Ms. R.: Why would you go home?
Ted: I'd get hungry.
Doug: I'd miss my mom and dad.
Rachel: Me too.
Ms. R.: Why do you think Max returned home?
Ted: I think he got tired of the wild things. They weren't very nice.
Doug: They kept roaring and gnashing their terrible teeth.
Rachel: I think he wanted to go home and be where someone loved him most.

By exploring what they would do if put in Max's situation, these readers are able to explore Max's motivation. Rachel, who most definitely would not want to stay with the wild things, is able to infer the motivation behind Max's return home.

She later put the following entry in her journal, "This is a story about a boy who acts wild. His mother sends him to bed without his supper. And then Max goes to where the wild things are. And then he starts a wild time. And then he sends the wild things to bed without their supper. And then he goes home and his mom forgives him and gives him supper. Moms always forgive you."

Rachel points out the critical episode that Sendak mentions. Rachel is confident that mothers love their children unconditionally. The anger that both Max and his mother express will be forgiven in the end.

Conclusion

Picture books are one of the mainstays in my first- and second-grade classroom. The children rely on the pictures more than as a way to decode text. They realize that a picture book is much more than a story with illustrations. For these readers, the picture book is an important marriage of picture and text. The pictures and illustrations work together to help them understand the essence of the author's message. A message, which no matter how fantastic, they are able to connect to their own experiences and their own lives. As they grow older, their experiences and lives will change, and rather than losing relevance for these older readers the picture books will bring them a new and perhaps wiser message.

Charlotte Huck writes, "Literature can take us out of ourselves and return us to ourselves—slightly different with each book we have loved" (Huck, 1990). When a community of learners is given the opportunity to study a body of literature and discuss and share their insights with one another they not only learn and change, they also grow from the connections they make between the different literary works and the insights and personal connections that the other members of the community share with them. They work together to build meaning and make sense of their reading.

WORKS CITED

Authors on Tape: Maurice Sendak. 1988. New York: Trumpet Club.

Huck, Charlotte. 1990. "The Power of Children's Literature in the Classroom." In Kathy Gnagey Short and Kathryn Mitchell Pierce (Eds.), *Talking about Books: Creating Literate Communities*. Portsmouth, NH: Heinemann.

Needham, Nancy. December, 1990. "Keeping the Magic Alive: Chris Van Allsburg." NEA *Today*, 9(4), 21.

4

Picture Books Let the Imagination Soar

Susan Benedict

> Dear Mrs. B.
>
> This unit on picture books is interesting, now that I'm ten. I never realized that picture books could be so fun! At first, I thought this unit would be BORING!! But now, reading books like *The Baby Uggs Are Hatching*, *Annabelle Swift, Kindergartener*, and *Sleeping Ugly* refresh my mind on what is was like to be a child.
>
> I had THOUSANDS of little golden books, Mercer Mayer books, and of course easy-to-read books. . . . My dad would read to me and I'd follow along. Like, if he said "Bugle," I'd put it in my head and memorize "bugle". . . . Picture books really helped me in my life. They let my imagination soar!
>
> Charley

My work with elementary students has revealed that many students quickly become proficient readers and by about age seven are requesting and seeking out thick books that resemble those that older children and adults read. In many quarters children like Charley have gotten on the "adult reading bus" (Smith, 1983) and have left a large body of children's literature behind them in the nursery. Although Charley's letter makes us smile, I find it a little sad that at ten, Charley and his peers might need to "refresh their minds on what it was like to be a child." Perhaps we need to slow the bus down, or at least to extend the route to some of the old neighborhoods. I am not advocating abolishing the wealth of juvenile and young adult fiction from the elementary schools, but rather suggesting that it be offered to our students with a good dose of picture books as well.

The literature has documented the importance of helping students make reading and writing connections (Atwell 1987, Calkins 1991, Chew 1985, Graves 1990, Hansen 1987, Murray 1986, Newkirk 1989, Rief 1992, Rosenblatt 1978,). We have learned to encourage children to make reading and writing connections, but more often than not we provide adult models of literature in the novel format. The length, complexity of story lines, and variety of picture books make them an ideal model for young student writers. A teacher during reading aloud, or students during reading time can read many times the number of picture books than longer texts. This provides the reader or listener with a concentrated opportunity to examine an individual author's or illustrator's work, compare the work of several authors, explore a genre, and sample the wide range of possibilities available to writers.

In the pages that follow, my fifth-grade students speak about their experiences with picture books through their written and spoken words. Together we spent eight weeks reading, savoring, analyzing, and writing picture books. We also identified topics to research. These children, who already knew that authors write about what they know, expanded what they knew. Finally, we studied the authors themselves. We poured over book jackets, biographies, articles, and promotional material, looking for any shred of information we could find on authors we imagined could be our writing teachers. We read our authors' books to ourselves, to our friends, and to the whole class. We recorded our observations. In the end we shared our findings with the entire school. Here is our story.

On a cold, Monday morning in February my twenty-five students and I began our reading period in the reading well in the school library. We sat in a circle. This was something new. We had never begun our reading time together in the library. The students wondered why we were there. I had brought two books to talk about: Kathryn Lasky's *Sea Swan* and Peter Parnall's *Apple Tree*. I explained why I had chosen the two books to read during our reading time that day. I had read Lasky's *Sugaring Time*, and knew of her longer texts. I said I loved her control of language. The way she used words made me reread passages and wish I could harness language with the same facility. I said I was surprised to find a picture book written by her—I didn't know she wrote picture books. I had chosen *Apple Tree* because I had read *Winter Barn*, and had marveled at how much activity Parnall could find in a barn in winter. His illustrations delighted me with their focus and simplicity.

I was looking forward to the next forty-five minutes, when I could read these two books. I told my students that I hoped they too would find picture books they would enjoy. Before I turned them loose on the collection,

I suggested we come back together and share what we had found at the end of the period. No one looked at the clock. We never made it to recess that day or the next. Our investigation of picture books had begun.

We spent a week reading, sharing, and reflecting in our reading journals. Unlike our established uninterupted, silent, sustained reading time, our picture book time had acquired an almost constant buzz. Children who had read all year in isolation now indulged in Dr. Seuss, Maculay, Sendak, Van Allsburg, Rylant, Kellogg, Fox, and scores of others with their friends and peers. Others weren't quite so sure they wanted to read picture books.

> Dear Mrs. B.
>
> . . . The only thing that bugs me about reading picture books is that they're so young and meant for young kids.
>
> Sean

The reading spurred opinion. Jennifer was disturbed that Yolen had "messed" with *The Sleeping Beauty*. "I think that it isn't a great idea to turn a story around. I like the pictures better than the text. I don't like the book. I don't like the way she tells it." On the other hand, Charley found *Sleeping Ugly* hilarious. He said, "I particularly like how Yolen mixes the past and the present. Time really speeds up toward the end. Look at the T-shirts the kids are wearing."

My students were talking about books and swapping books as they had never done before. Jessica took picture books home to read to her little brother. She let us know some books weren't really well received by little kids. "These ideas are too hard," she said. "Jacob didn't really understand *The Magic School Bus Inside the Earth*. It was hard to get him to listen to the story." After Jessica read this book to the class, it was difficult for students to get their hands on any of Joanna Cole's Magic School Bus books. Differences of opinions like Charley's and Jennifer's, as well as rave reviews, put some books on everyone's reading list.

From my closet I took two boxes of books I had in my classroom when I was teaching the early primary grades. Children reread *Goodnight Moon*, by Margaret Wise Brown, and *The Carrot Seed*, by Ruth Krauss, saying, "I remember this." "Oh, this was my favorite book." This unit reacquainted old friends. Charley wrote:

> Dear Mrs. B.
>
> I just finished three picture books; I was interested in *Gorky Rises* [William Steig] because my mother said that this book was given to me by my grandparents, yet I never read it. I found

it very good. Gorky almost drifted into space with his formula. What formula? You'll have to read it to find out!

Charley

The students began to look at old favorites with a new vision:

Dear Mrs. B.

I read *Mike Mulligan and His Steam Shovel* by Virginia Lee Burton and illustrated by her too. This book always made me kind of sad that they couldn't get out of the cellar that they dug. But they were happy, and if they are happy, I guess it's okay.

Her pictures aren't really detailed but kind of nice. They are to me fluffy and give me a good feeling. They aren't really jagged like real life looks. But she's really accurate about the colors. The colors and expressions really let you see the characters. I really love one picture—the sun is barely up and one eye is over the horizon.

I think that sometimes it might be better to have the same person draw the pictures and write the book because the author would know what they wanted it to look like. The pictures would go better with the story.

'Til next time . . .

Evan

Stacey became interested in Barbara Cooney. Cooney's illustrations for *Miss Rumphius* and *Island Boy* had drawn her in. She began combing the school and local library for books written and/or illustrated by Cooney. Finding *The Ox-Cart Man*, written by Donald Hall, delighted her. She was surprised to discover Rumer Godden's *The Story of Holly and Ivy* in her collection at home. For the first time Stacey took note of who wrote and illustrated the books she read.

After reading broadly, the students focused their reading on specific authors and topics. They recorded their findings and their observations. Sean began reading anything that had Maurice Sendak's name on it.

Dear Mrs. B.

Today I read three Maurice Sendak books. This is the man I want to be my author very much. The three books I read were *Pierre*, *Chicken Soup with Rice*, and *Alligators All Around*, which were all published in the same year. My favorite book that he wrote is *One Was Johnny*.

Sean

Several days later Sean once again recorded his observations.

> Dear Mrs. B.
>
> I really like the book *Outside Over There* by Maurice Sendak. The illustrations are really good. Sometimes pictures in the background tell other stories in this book.
>
> Sean

While he was reading Sendak, Sean decided that he really wanted to know more about mountains. He said he liked to ski, and he really liked looking at mountains, but that he knew very little else about mountains. He began looking to see if Sendak knew anything about mountains.

> Dear Mrs. B.
>
> I think the only time Sendak draws either mountains or some kind of vegetation, he draws it best and prefers water colors. I do too because it looks better, and you can blend the colors in better. In the book *Outside Over There* Sendak tried to avoid drawing bigger mountains. Today I read *Outside Over There* again. I looked at some of the pictures a lot (the ones that had mountains in them). Some of the pictures were very well illustrated. Another thing I saw about the book is that all the pictures with the mother of the baby are all bright and shiny. I also read a book by Thomas Locker called *Where the River Begins*. The mountains in those pictures were really good. I couldn't even tell what kind of material he used to draw the pictures with. . . .
>
> Sean

> Dear Mrs. B.
>
> Today for the second time I read *Mr. Rabbit and the Lovely Present* [Charlotte Zolotow] and *Outside Over There* for the third time to compare pictures. If you compare *Mr. Rabbit* to *Outside*, it has completely different pictures. But when you compare *Pierre* to *One Was Johnny*, *Alligators All Around*, and *Chicken Soup with Rice*, they're really all the same but just a different story. And when you compare *Where the Wild Things Are* to *In The Night Kitchen* they are also different. I think Sendak has totally different writing and pictures.
>
> Sean

Sean realized that looking at pictures of mountains in picture books wasn't going to significantly expand his knowledge about mountains. The notion of expanding what he knew by collecting new information was new to him. He found the need to look at what others were doing as he researched his topic. I shared some of the work I had been doing with the class. In addition to his picture books, I also read Parnall's *The Day Watchers*. In-service work I'd been doing with my colleagues at the time had me thinking about trees. Just as Barbara Cooney's illustrations had invited Stacey in, so too had I initially been drawn to Parnall's work through his illustrations. I told the class these things and shared notes from my journal.

Dear Class,

The Day Watchers by Peter Parnall: Each story or chapter is based on personal experience. What experiences do I have with trees?

1. cutting the white birch
2. Walt Hall's cider press
3. drinking cider from the cellar at West Hill
4. childhood tree house in the white pine
5. observing tree silhouette in late winter at sunset
6. growth of trees—those white pine overrunning our yard
7. Ash tree outside my kitchen window
8. power of a dead tree, splitting logs
9. Alice and Arbor Day

My experiences aren't as deep/memorable as Parnall's seem to be. I might not write about the experiences but rather just put it into the mill.

I'm struck by this idea of apple trees, but Parnall has done a book on apple trees—how can I compete? If I choose to, how can I make it different enough to make it mine and not a poor imitation of his?

Mrs. B.

Sean found he could not directly relate others' thinking into writing strategies that would work for him. He found he would need to wrestle through to solutions that worked for him.

Dear Mrs. B.

Today you read some of your journal entries on your topic trees. I think that I probably won't have enough experiences with mountains to write a detailed story, but I'll try. The only

> really good experiences are: I ski a lot; I've been to Mt. Washington once; I really read a lot on mountains. But on the other hand I think I'll have enough facts to go on because when we went to the library, Mrs. Lincoln showed us how to use the indexes and the *National Geographic Index* had about three pages on mountains. So I guess I'll have enough.
>
> Sean

I wrote back.

> Dear Sean,
>
> I know what you mean that you don't feel you have a lot of experience. So often I look at what authors write about and feel nothing happens to me that measures up to this! Or I don't seem to look at the world with the same intensity as these writers. I think we need to each find our own way into the stories we have to tell. I know I struggle with that problem all the time. I'll let you know how my decisions are coming, and I'll be interested to hear what's working for you.
>
> Mrs. B.

Sean gives us a partial glimpse at some of his writing decisions through subsequent journal entries.

> I'm going to try to write my story. One of the goals I'm going to try to fulfill is planning the story out like an author and a lot of describing the scene.
>
> I'm starting my story today. It's about a bobcat that lives in the mountains. John [a fellow student and friend whose topic was bobcats] and I are working on it. I'm also quite happy on how I started my story. We haven't decided on a title yet though.
>
> I really like the book *The Hat* [Tomi Ungerer], but I really don't think I'm going to try a book that repeats itself like that book.
>
> I have decided to not do my book with John because it will probably be easier not to. We have different opinions on how the book is made.
>
> I really didn't find a whole lot of information on mountains. But I found out that my author has written or illustrated over forty books that I know of. I stopped counting after that. He

> had the most awards and publications for the book *Where the Wild Things Are*. I think he also illustrated more than he wrote. I'm going to read it to the group.

Along the way Sean and I looked at parts of *The Art of Maurice Sendak* together. I showed him how the book was organized. He was fascinated to learn that *Where the Wild Things Are* was originally going to be *Where the Wild Horses Are*, but Sendak reported that he didn't feel he could successfully draw horses. He also read about some of Sendak's experiences that related to *Outside Over There*. He learned that Ida was a conglomerate of the girl on the Morton Salt label, a little girl in a book Sendak read as a child whose boots filled with rain water, and Sendak's sister. Sean had seen the girl on the Morton Salt label and could see her resemblance to Ida.

> I'm trying to start my story over. Instead of a bobcat as the main character it's a little boy who wanders off.

At the same time he was pulling together the things he had learned from Sendak. He said, "To catch people's attention you can make a book funny—not quite in the text but more in the pictures. You don't have to have exquisite pictures but more funny ones." Sean felt that creating a picture book was within his grasp. Sendak had given him that confidence. He became Sean's silent writing partner. Together they began Sean's story, *Baby Gerber*. (See Figure 4–1.) A reader can read a great deal into a writer's writing. One can't help but wonder about the relationship between Gerber foods and Morton Salt; Spud's rescue of Baby Gerber and Ida's of her sister; a preoccupied mother reading letters in the arbor and a sleeping mother; a father at work and a father at sea. A reader could easily guess what inspired Sean to incorporate conversation balloons in his writing after reading *In the Night Kitchen*. Sean wrote with confidence. He had spent more than a month reading, thinking, sketching, and researching before he began drafting.

Evan's story is different from Sean's. He too was faced with reading and writing decisions. His journal entries probably tell the story best.

> Dear Mrs. B.
>
> I just read and studied a wonderful book titled *Moon Song* by Byrd Baylor and illustrated by Ronald Himler. This book really gives you a feeling about what Baylor thought about why the coyote howled at the moon. I really love Himler's illustrations. They are like charcoal pencil. I really want to try to do this medium. If it's good, it looks really wonderful. The story makes

FIGURE 4–1: *Sean's Baby Gerber Story*

> you think a little bit about what Baylor is trying to say. But when you find it out, it's a really great story. I love the idea.
>
> Evan

Then Evan discovered a number of books on which Baylor and Parnall collaborated. He read *Desert Voices*, *Everybody Needs a Rock*, *Hawk, I Am Your Brother*, and *The Way to Start a Day*. He said, "Baylor and Parnall must really study the desert. He knows where the shadows are at different times of day. I really love Parnall's illustrations. He draws the pictures and they go along with the poem like roasting marshmallows and camping go together."

Evan began to devour anything he could find written by Baylor. He was delighted when I discovered *And It Is Still That Way*. He noted the central role the desert played in much of her poetry. He knew about the desert and wanted to know more,

> Dear Mrs. B.
>
> I read *If You Are a Hunter of Fossils*. This book is kind of different. It goes back several million years ago and then comes to today. In my head it looks like a zig zag. But Baylor taught me that it's really just one big cycle. Baylor, I learned, writes about things she likes to do and she knows about those things because she does them. Why write about something you aren't interested in? Baylor half studies and half knows and it shows in her great books. She always thinks about what happened ago and what is going to happen.
>
> I just read *I'm in Charge of Celebrations*. . . . I bet people do ask her if she gets lonely out there. I would laugh too. I wonder why Byrd doesn't illustrate her own books. Parnall's go with them well, but I just wonder.
>
> Evan

While Evan read Baylor, he also read factual information about the desert. His notes began to stack up. He began to wonder how he would pull all of these things together.

> Dear Mrs. B.
>
> I have so many ideas for books now. I think I know what I'm going to do. I like to read the books Baylor writes and I get ideas, but I don't think I could write a book like her. It just doesn't feel right to me.

I wrote back.

Dear Evan,

I'd be interested to hear about your ideas. It may be useful to explore some of your ideas in writing in this journal.

Of course, you can't write a book like Baylor. You're not Baylor, but I expect there are some things that she does or she makes you think about that you might try out. I'd like to hear about what you're learning; that may help your writing.

Mrs. B.

Dear Mrs. B.

I was going to make a story where a kangaroo rat and a coyote were the lion and the mouse—kind of like that. I thought that was a good idea. I could try, but I don't think it would come out too well. I've never been very good at poem like writing. Maybe I could try to learn. I'd like it to sound so beautiful . . . I just noticed she does put facts into her books. Like if you smell a rock it has its special smell. You don't really think about that, but it is very true when you do it. I want to try to put a little Baylor into my story, but not a lot because that would mess it up.

Evan

Dear Evan

I think that you should look at this as an opportunity to try something new. If you don't want to try poetry for your picture book, maybe you could try writing a poem about the desert for yourself. I'd be happy to help you out if you like. Let me know.

Mrs. B.

Along the way, I shared more about what I was observing and learning from my study of Peter Parnall because I felt if my students reflected on their observations, their very reflections might lead the way into their own writing and illustrating.

Dear Class,

There seems to be a distinct difference between the books Parnall writes and illustrates and those he just illustrates. When he illustrates his own texts, he seems to get closer to his subject. The drawings seem more detailed and focused. I get the feeling that Parnall has just left the spot the drawing is depicting. This increased focus seems to have also developed over time. For example, his drawings in *Alfalfa Hill*, which is one of his earlier books, are more cluttered than the illustrations in *Apple Tree*. In the latter book he brought me right up to the tree so that I could see the insect holes and the chickadee's tail sticking out of a hole just big enough for a nest.

Parnall's writing strikes a better balance for me with his illustrations in his most recent books. *Alfalfa Hill*, for example, seems to be a literal translation of the text into illustration or illustration into text. In *Apple Tree* both the text and illustrations contain images not even suggested in the other. This seems to me to be a better marriage between text and pictures.

Parnall seems to be looking increasingly closely at his subjects. It's interesting that he dedicated one of his latest books to "Byrd who helps us see" (1988). Parnall certainly has learned to "see." He sees things I never even knew were there to see in the first place:

- tightly woven grasses, all uniform in size, that comprise a robin's nest;
- ravens are the first to know when apples are ripe;
- mice paths formed in the fall will be tunnels when the snow falls;
- some flies pretend to be bees to scare away their enemies;
- it's not the north but the northwest side where moss and lichens grow;
- mosquitoes sometimes lay their eggs in crevices of trees that are filled with rain water.

If Parnall has learned to see, he has taught me to look.

Mrs. B.

In time Evan synthesized his observations of Baylor's writing:

- Most of her books are illustrated by Peter Parnall;
- She writes very short sentences;
- She also loves to write about celebrations;
- Her writing is very peaceful and happy;
- She would have had to go out in the desert and observe everything or she could not describe and write as well as she does;
- She likes to write about animals;
- From her books I've noticed she's very aware and sees a lot of neat things that unaware people miss.

FIGURE 4–2: *Sample Pages from Evan's* The Desert's Children

And then Evan wrote. See Figure 4–2 for samples pages from his picture book.

Eight weeks later, the activity in the classroom reached a fevered pitch. We opened windows so we wouldn't be asphyxiated by rubber cement. Jennifer struggled with her pen and ink drawings. Dave measured pages so that his text and illustrations wouldn't end up in the gutter that made up his binding. Stacey sat correcting missed spelling errors with white out. Melanie's brow furrowed as she puzzled over the organization of her author display. Contact paper protected pages that had been created through research, imagination, revision, and hard work. As the first volumes were completed, those published students became instant experts ready to help the next ones finish. Some were expert contacters, others gluers, stitchers, or organizers. Parents delivered children with large author displays that had been polished at home.

The library opened its doors to receive the writing of our in-house authors. As the children finished, they each brought their author displays to the library, located all the authors' books in the library, and carefully arranged their displays with the books their authors had written. These displays were invitations to the rest of the school to read and enjoy the books as we had. In a specially designated display rack each student placed his own published picture book.

On the last Friday in April we sat or stood, alone or in groups of two or three, savoring the work we'd done. We had seen all of this work in progress, but today it was different: polished and completed. Students scrutinized the work in hushed tones. They awarded a reverence to these pages that they hadn't even given books of renowned authors and illustrators. Silently they wrote messages to their peers to share what they saw and appreciated.

Later the students reflected on their individual journeys.

> Dear Mrs. B.
>
> I don't know where to start. I think this was a really wonderful thing to do. I learned the most from my author display, but I also learned a lot about the desert for my picture book. I think this went very well for me. I've learned to write this flowing poetry. To write of things you like, and personal experiences. I've learned to write more peaceful words and how to write this different but pretty style of poetry.
>
> I didn't think I would get all of this done because I started [writing] so late. I get so panicked, but you know me and due dates. I definitely think you should do this same project next year because the kids will learn a lot and have fun. I sure had fun doing my picture book and author display. I think the students liked it because we could choose our own topic. I think that made a difference. It went really well for me. I always like to learn about authors and I think the author display was a great way to do it.
>
> Evan

And I reflected too.

> The past eight weeks have been filled with so many tangible and intangible results. My students have established and sharpened their literary analysis skills. For example, Evan now writes about everything he reads with a critical eye to how the author created an effect, made a point, moved a story along, or said something important. I can't help but feel the time he

spent lingering over Baylor's language gave him the confidence both to applaud and examine what he reads. He feels he is a writer now. I remember in September how fearful Evan was that his words and ideas would not match and could not add up to the books he read. He sometimes avoided writing. And Sean, who always wrote with a touch of wit, now feels he's an illustrator; Sendak did that for him.

Not all of my students are comfortable with the language arts. This study gave students like Dave the opportunity to reflect upon the marriage between words and pictures. He broke out of some of the more traditional page designs, and, instead, created a fluid relationship between the story in pictures and the story in text. He, perhaps more than anyone else, really internalized what a picture book is.

I'd often worried about my students' oral reading. The past eight weeks gave them real opportunities to orally interpret literature to their peer audience. Jessica's dramatic and skillful reading of *The Magic School Bus: Journey to the Center of the Earth* inspired others to strive for similar responses to their oral presentations. I can't help but think back to the many private conversations students had with me and with each other about the books they were reading and the books they were writing. They listened intently to each other and learned to ask the questions and offer the comments that would help their peers and themselves to discover and write their intended meanings. Their journal entries showed increasing insight. As they responded to my letters, they and I were challenged to explore more deeply and examine with increased intensity the books we read. Their entries showed their capacities to compare and contrast writing styles and characters' motivations. They identified plots and themes. They made connections between my mini-lessons and what they understood about their own work. They explored those connections and their writing plans in their journals.

In addition to their picture books, the students wrote second pieces about their researched topics. It was gratifying to see their abilities to develop their library and research skills in locating specific information, as well as see how far and wide their research carried them. Final projects and pieces demonstrated that my students had learned to use vertical files, reference books, the card catalog, and periodicals in the school and town library. They'd learned to take notes and to sift and categorize information. They experimented with genre.

Their writing included poetry, fiction, informational nonfiction, letters, historical fiction, and folk literature.

They had chosen their teachers well: the authors and illustrators of picture books.

WORKS CITED

Atwell, Nancie. 1987. *In the Middle: Writing, Reading, and Learning with Adolescents*. Portsmouth, NH: Boynton/Cook.

Calkins, Lucy McCormick. 1991. *Living Between the Lines*. Portsmouth, NH: Heinemann.

Chew, Charles. 1985. "Instruction Can Link Reading and Writing." In Jane Hansen, Thomas Newkirk, and Donald Graves (Eds.), *Breaking Ground*. Portsmouth, NH: Heinemann.

Graves, Donald H. 1990. *Discover Your Own Literacy*. Portsmouth, NH: Heinemann.

Hansen, Jane. 1987. *When Writers Read*. Portsmouth, NH: Heinemann.

Lanes, Selma G. 1980. *The Art of Maurice Sendak*. New York: Abrams.

Murray, Donald M. 1986. *Read to Write*. New York: Holt, Rinehart and Winston.

Newkirk, Thomas. 1989. *More Than Stories: The Range of Children's Writing*. Portsmouth, NH: Heinemann.

Rief, Linda. 1992. *Seeking Diversity: Language Arts with Adolescents*. Portsmouth, NH: Heinemann.

Rosenblatt, Louise. 1978. *The Reader, the Text, and the Poem*. Carbondale, IL: Southern Illinois University.

Smith, Frank. 1983. "Reading and Writing Club." Address at the Maine Reading Association Conference, Bangor, Maine.

Picture Books: An Easy Place to Think

5

Lenore Reilly Carlisle

Carrying a box full of picture books, I headed toward the sixth-grade classroom where I was to meet seven students with whom I would be working. As a language arts resource teacher in a large elementary school, I have opportunities to work with students and teachers in what sometimes seems an endless variety of ways. Some are rather mundane. Others are quite extraordinary. I find it exciting to work with children of all ages and of different ability levels. One moment I may be working with a group of emergent first-grade readers who seem to be struggling, and in the next I'll be working with a classroom teacher to plan a unit on mythology for highly proficient fifth graders. On this particular day, I would be working on a project to which I'd really been looking forward.

As I walked down the hallway, I wondered about the students I would be working with over the next several days. Would there be some with whom I had worked last year? Or would I be faced with a totally new crop? I wondered for a particular reason. My plan for working with them might seem a bit out of the ordinary to students I had not worked with before. But to some of the old timers, I wouldn't have to explain why the only things I had with me were a pile of picture books and a few questions to ask about them.

What I ended up with was the best of both worlds—some familiar faces, some new—in all, seven eager sixth graders of varying ability levels waiting to see what our time together would turn into. Before I even had a chance to go into my long song and dance about why I had only picture books with me and why picture books can and should be read by students of all ages, one of the old timers began to explain. Jonathan, always ready with information to help shape any group's opinion, began with a little chiding.

Jonathan: What do you have, Mrs. Carlisle? Typical sixth-grade reading material? *Good Night Moon*? *Where the Wild Things Are*?

Jonathan and I had worked on a special project together when he was in fourth grade. One of those early readers who had read practically everything I'd ever heard of and then some, Jonathan was begging for something out of the ordinary to work on. After a lot of negotiating, I had decided to capitalize on his dramatic flare and give him a chance to do dramatic readings and tape record all of Chris Van Allsburg's books for second graders who were involved in an author study of Van Allsburg. Part way into the venture, we had abandoned the recordings and taken off on a psychological and philosophical study of Van Allsburg's work. So here was Jonathan, ready to embark upon another stroll through the world of picture books.

Before I could begin to tell the students what we'd be doing, a loud sigh rose from the masses. It was Matthew.

Matthew: Picture books? Oh don't tell me this is one of those things where we're going to sit around and talk about how artistic all the illustrations are and about how Humpty Dumpty was really a story about politics.

Hmm, this might be tough. This student's mother was a librarian. She'd obviously tried some of my tricks. But Jonathan came to the rescue.

Jonathan: No, no. Matthew, it's neat. She asks all these insane questions about things that happen in the books. It's philosophical stuff. You think it's going to be dumb but it isn't. At least it wasn't dumb last time.

"Insane questions"? "At least it wasn't dumb last time"? I think that's what is usually referred to as damming with faint praise. But I was relieved nonetheless not to have had to begin the period with a long defense.

Jonathan was right in assuming that I'd want to look at philosophical issues in the books, or at least to engage in philosophical inquiry as a way of going about getting at some of the most significant issues in a book. It's part of a project I worked on with Gareth Matthews, professor of philosophy at the University of Massachusetts. Matthews has long been an admirer of children and their fluid intellects. A sometimes critic of those developmentalists who might otherwise overlook capacities in a child that cannot easily be measured (such as philosophical thinking), Matthews saw in children a natural inquisitiveness that he felt deserved to be encouraged. He suggested that one of the only groups of people who truly honor the capacity of the child for critical, creative, and philosophical thinking, is children's book writers.

> If Piaget, the first great psychologist of cognitive development and perhaps the only great one, isn't sensitive to philosophical thinking in young children, who is? . . . The answer may come as a surprise. It is writers—at least some writers—of children's stories who have been almost the only important adults to recognize that many children are naturally intrigued by many philosophical questions. (Matthews, 1980)

Matthews had spent years talking to children and reading books with them, exploring such topics as the question of the weakness of the will and the compatibility of determinism and the notion of free will in Arnold Lobel's "Cookies" (*Frog and Toad Together*); and being and nonbeing, dreaming and skepticism, appearance and reality and the foundations of knowledge in Frank Tashlin's *The Bear that Wasn't*. When he asked if I'd be interested in working on a project with him that would result in a series of questions to be used in conjunction with some wonderful picture books, I jumped at the opportunity. My role in the project was more or less as a consultant, trying out questions, finding out if stories were appealing, and determining whether children could sustain a discussion without a lot of adult intervention or reinforcement of right or wrong answers. At any rate, we eventually developed series of questions to go along with several different picture books (Wise Owl, 1989).

While the questions were originally aimed at the K–3 population, I was fairly certain they would stimulate discussion among these sixth graders. For this particular group of sixth graders, I had chosen the book *I Know a Lady* by Charlotte Zolotow. It is a simply written book, a twenty-four-page spread with relatively little text. It presents a glimpse of the relationship between a child and an elderly neighbor. The old woman remains nameless, but her kindness to those around her is clear, and there can be little doubt that her good deeds have meaning. I chose the book because I knew the students were soon to begin a unit on aging and the elderly, and I thought this might raise some issues that would be relevant to novels they'd later be discussing with their classroom teacher.

During our first meeting, we talked about the experiences students had had with elderly relatives and neighbors. I asked them to think about what their relationships with elderly people were like. Drawing upon some cooperative learning strategies, I asked the students to pair off and spend two minutes talking about a positive interaction or experience they had had with an elderly person and two minutes talking about a difficult or uncomfortable experience with an elderly person. Each partner got to share these two things. We then came together, shared some of what we'd heard, and began to list words that had emerged frequently during the discussion. Awkward, tender, sweet, sad, heart breaking, wise, old fashioned, stubborn, dependent, and independent were some of the recurring terms.

Then I let them loose with picture books: *Now One Foot, Now the Other* and *Nana Upstairs and Nana Downstairs* by Tomie DePaola; *Wilfred Gordon MacDonald Partridge* by Mem Fox; and *Annie and the Old One* by Miska Miles. I wanted the students to see that the elderly could be portrayed in a number of very different ways in literature. Fortunately, picture books provided the economy necessary to convey this message to the students quickly and intelligently.

When we met the following day, the students continued to read until they had each read all four books. I asked the students to reflect upon how the books presented situations or feelings similar to those they had experienced with elderly people. All of the students expressed great admiration for the way in which the books captured and explored realistic aspects of the lives of elderly people. They were at once touched by the kindness and wisdom they saw in some of the characterizations (*Annie and the Old One*) and disturbed by the harsh realities of aging found in other stories (*Nana Upstairs and Nana Downstairs, Wilfred Gordon MacDonald Partridge* and *Now One Foot, Now the Other*).

The students had seen for themselves that many picture books contain more than simple illustration and text for very young children. Two students, Eva and Katie, even went so far as to suggest that these particular picture books "probably shouldn't be read by kids until they're in at least fourth grade." Jonathan proclaimed *Wilfred Gordon MacDonald Partridge* "a classic." By now, I was convinced that the group was ready to focus their attention on a single book. I handed out copies of *I Know A Lady* and asked each student to read it carefully, thoughtfully. For some, that meant slowly reading each page and studying the illustrations. For others, it meant reading through the book two or three times over. One student could be heard sub-vocalizing, possibly feeling that the words would offer up more meaning if they were read aloud. David, who had read through the book at lightning speed, looked up at me inquisitively and with great puzzlement asked, "What are we supposed to see? There's nothing here."

It wasn't necessary for me to respond. Josh, usually soft spoken, was the first to disagree.

Josh: Are you kidding? This book is full of stuff.

David: Where?

Josh: All through it. Like the way the old lady does things for people and that keeps her from being lonely. And the way she feeds the milk to the cat, how she's kind.

Eva: I think it was sad how she lived, so alone and everything.

Katie: It really doesn't say much about that. I mean she might have lived alone her whole life pretty much. She might have really liked that. I mean she got to do pretty much whatever she wanted. Nobody said, "Don't have all those kids in all the time." I can just hear my grandfather saying that to my grandmother. She'd have us over there morning, noon and night, but my grandfather likes peace and quiet.

Jonathan: I got the sense that she was lonely. Not every minute of every day. Cause she had things she liked to do that weren't, well she wasn't always trying to get people around her. When she gardened. You feel like she liked that anyway.

Eva: I completely missed that part. Where?

(Jonathan finds page, shows her.)

Jonathan: See her face. She looks happy enough.

Eva: Yeah. I guess I was so into thinking she was so lonely. Probably because there's this old lady on our street, and she always wants us to come in and she asks, "What did you learn in school today?" which isn't the easiest question to answer.

At this point, I could see that the students had lighted upon some of the issues and questions I wanted to pursue with them. In particular I wanted to explore with them their understanding of intergenerational relationships and their awareness of different life-styles.

Carlisle: Let's talk for a minute about the old woman in the story. Eva, was it you? and I think Jonathan who felt that the old lady felt sad, lonely.

Eva: I still think she felt lonely, sort of sad. Even when she's smiling in the illustrations, it's the watery kind of smile, you know, sort of. . . .

David: It's like she's yearning. The author should have said, "She waved at the children as they went to school and smiled a yearning and longing smile."

Katie: Oh my god! Everybody thinks she's so desperate. I read the whole thing, and I never even thought she was sad once. I mean compare it to the other stuff we read. There were some really sad cases there, like the one tied in the chair so she wouldn't fall out [*Nana Upstairs and Nana Downstairs*]. I mean that's sad.

Jonathan: But was it sad to her? Even there it didn't say she hated her life. She might have said, "Hey, I'm ninety-four, I fall a lot, and they're doing me a favor to tie me in and keep me from falling."

On the surface this might sound like the typical argumentative banter that is bound to take place whenever you ask two sixth graders to give their independent views about a book. Upon closer inspection, however, we see that the students have entered into some rather remarkable dialogue. David seems to be grappling with what it means to be old, what it means to yearn, and what it means to be sad. Are old people inevitably sad because they are old?

And when Jonathan asks, "But was it sad to her?", he's really trying to point out that David and Eva are offering a subjective judgement. But he pushes even further, making the whole group embark upon a dialogue wherein they begin to explore whether indeed there can be such a thing as objective sadness, with Katie eventually arriving at the conclusion that no, nothing can be sad in and of itself. It is always part of the subjective perception.

Also worth noting is the way so many of the students are able to consider alternative perspectives. Jonathan, for example, moves right into the old woman's psyche when he says, "Hey, I'm ninety-four. . . ." Eva does something similar when she points out to the group that how a person perceives herself might not be a perfect match with someone else's perception.

Matthew: That's sort of true. We might feel sad reading about them, or looking at the pictures, and by the way I don't think her smile was "watery" and "longing." Where was I?

Eva: You were trying to make the point how the person feels might not be the same as what we feel. Like what we feel about them.

Jonathan: It's really right. I mean, when you're really little, you don't know how dumb you are, so you don't really mind the way adults treat you all the time, like you have half a brain. And when you're old, you probably don't know either.

Carlisle: So who knows best, Jonathan? Do we know best because we're older than very little kids and younger than very old people?

Jonathan: Well, it's hard to say whose knowledge is best. You can never really come to a conclusion on that one.

Eva: It's an impossible question.

Carlisle: What makes it impossible?

David: Well you can't say a kid is wrong about something when they think . . . hmm . . . well if they think there's something to be scared of, it doesn't matter if there's nothing there. They *know* they're scared. No matter what you say. That kid is going to be scared no matter what. So they're right for them. But not really right about it, about that there's something to be scared of, you know, from my view point.

Here they had embarked on an impressive and highly sophisticated discussion of whether or not knowledge can be valid within its own context. How do we assess what is good knowledge or real knowledge? What after all is knowledge? Is partial or subjective knowledge wrong by virtue of the fact that it is partial? In validating the feelings of a frightened young child, David seems to be suggesting to his peers that it is not.

Eva: Wait, this lady in the story isn't tied into a chair. She knows how she feels.

Josh: But when you're old, you could get to the point where you accept stuff.

Carlisle: Say some more about that, Josh. How does that connect with what Eva was saying?

Josh: This is hard to keep track of.

Jonathan: I know what you were saying. Do you want me to say it?

Josh: Yeah, yeah.

Jonathan: He's saying that being old and seeing yourself get all worn out in some ways, it might not be so sad, even if you realize it, because it's like the most natural thing in the world. First Ethel gets arthritis and Sarah loses her husband and everybody around you. . . .

Eva: You sound just like my grandmother! She's always telling us about all the things going wrong with her friends.

Jonathan: Wait, let me finish that. It's that after a while, you start to see it's all going to be over with. Like when you're six, you expect to lose your teeth. When you're eighty, you lose your friends.

The students touched upon questions that have kept many of us up at night. They were able to identify those odd commonalities that connect the very young and the very old. As they talked about life cycles and how some stages are more alike than we might initially think, they thought and asked questions in ways that made it evident to me that they were growing more confident at being able to deal with ambiguity. David asked if an elderly aunt's death was any less sad simply because it was part of the "natural order of stuff." Josh seemed to resonate with this concern, asking "Yeah, it's like is all this death made all right just because it's natural?" Matthew believed it was in fact all right, "But that doesn't mean it's any less sad." The following day Katie began the discussion before everyone had even assembled.

Katie: That's awful what you said about all your teeth come out if you're a kid and your friends die if you're old. That was sort of sick Jonathan.

Jonathan: It isn't sick. We were talking about if it's sad, well if it's sad to live alone, right? Wasn't that what we were talking about? That's just what I'm saying, that it isn't the most sad thing in the world. Don't you think it's possible to not be sad about that by the time you're seventy or something?

Matthew: He's right. It isn't so awful.

Carlisle: Jenny, what do you think? Is it so awful?

Jenny: It could be or it might not be. This woman, I don't think being old is so awful for her in the story.

During this part of the discussion the students frequently linked acceptance with wisdom. I asked them to talk about those two things, about how they might be connected. Jenny raised a question that then dominated several minutes of discussion. It was wonderful to see how she had gotten into the spirit of the kind of question I had been throwing at them. In essence her question asked whether wisdom and acceptance come as a result of hardship or whether they are something we can all hope to attain by virtue of our growing old. I thought that we might have come to the end of productive discussion. They seemed exhausted. I knew I was. But Katie wouldn't quit.

Katie: Were we talking about if she was sad? Because I'm the one who said I don't think she seems sad.
Jenny: That's what I think too. I agree with what you said.

It was clear they wanted to work more on that one. I convinced them to hold off, explaining that they all needed a little distance from today's thoughts. I asked them to bring the books home and read the story again. When we met the next day I decided to open the discussion with a completely different question. They gave my question a cursory treatment, then moved the discussion right back to the questions that had been puzzling them all along: Who feels sad here anyway? Is it us? Is it she? Is anybody really right?

Carlisle: Is it easy for people to live alone?
David: It could be, or it could not be. Depends what kind of shape they're in, and where they live, all sorts of stuff. If they drive, if they live far out of town.
Eva: Well this woman seems to have friends in the neighborhood. She seems to be able to get groceries because she's always baking and she gets stuff for her garden. She likes kids.
David: I still say there's something sad about the old lady.
Jonathan: Now we're right back to where we started. Is she sad or are we sad? She seems fine! I think we're sad because to us she looks all alone, and we start to think, "Hey maybe someday I'll be totally completely by myself like her, and I'll be rounding up the kiddies to feed them Oreos." But I don't think there's one thing in the entire book that makes you one hundred percent sure that she's sad.
David: I feel like we're reading a different book.
Eva: It's making me crazy. Like we're not getting the idea, I mean, me, David, is there anybody else that thinks this old lady is lonely?
Josh: I didn't say she's never lonely. I just don't think that the book is all about how sad old people are, that their life is all over. She's got plenty of good stuff, the kids, the strayed cat, the birds, the garden.
Katie: Hey! Hey, you know what? It could be that you're getting the idea she's lonely from the little girl, right? She's imagining the old woman was a little girl once.

Jenny: She doesn't imagine that. The old lady really was a little girl once.

Katie: But she does imagine it, doesn't she? What it was like? And she says the thing about "Oh, I wonder if she was a kid like me and did she know an old lady who gave out cookies." Find that page. [Finds page, reads it.]

Matthew: That's really good. You solved it. It's the kid that's afraid of being old and alone. Because everybody teaches kids that being alone is scary. On TV they make it seem, that, sort of if you're old then you don't, well nobody takes you seriously, they all abandon you or something.

Josh: Yeah, yeah. It's the little girl that's sad. Hey, Mrs. Carlisle, did we solve it?

Katie: Wait a minute. What was the question?

Eva: Were we supposed to solve something?

David: I still say the old woman is sad. How can you read this book and not think she's sad?

Jonathan: We can talk about this for days. You can talk about this for three days, you change you mind about seven times, and then you can't even remember what the question was.

Eva: I don't think there even was a question.

I sent the students back to class a few minutes late that day. In the days that followed we talked more about the book. We talked about when people get to make choices about their life-styles and about how often we don't get to make choices. We pondered gift giving and what it means to the giver and the receiver. We discussed gardens and why people tend them. And we talked about thinking. I shared some of my understanding of what it means to think critically and creatively. I talked about the etymology of the word "philosophy," explaining that it means "the love of wisdom." David claimed that at one point his head was pounding he was "thinking so hard." And Eva expressed an amazement and delight we all felt when she wrote in her evaluation of our time together, "I can't believe this one beensy book kept us talking for about six days."

A novelist may convey a message with perfection over three hundred pages. A poet may do it in ten lines. One artist may evoke an emotion through an intricate and detailed oil painting on a flat canvas. Another may evoke that same feeling through abstract three-dimensional form. And the writers and illustrators of picture books use their medium to evoke the same feelings, to convey the same messages within the confines of "one beensy book." We can't measure the effectiveness of one form against another. They each do what they do in their own unique way, and they all have their usefulness.

If we recognize the picture book as a legitimate art form and as a legitimate part of literature in general, then it seems only natural that we should return to the picture book genre as a place from which we will derive reason to be delighted, to be moved, to be amazed, or to feel any of the myriad emotions evoked in us by art and literature. Jenny, perhaps the most soft spoken member of our group, felt that picture books had given her a new perspective:

> I think I'll probably keep reading picture books. Not all the time, but sometimes. They're an easy place to think.

WORKS CITED

Matthews, Gareth. 1980. *Philosophy and the Young Child*. Cambridge, MA: Harvard University.

Wise Owl. 1989. Littleton, MA: Sundance.

Scribbling Down the Pictures

Tricia Crockett and Sara Weidhaas

"Hey, Mrs. Rief, why are all these picture books here?"

"Yeah, we're eighth graders now."

In the back corner of the room a thick rug covered the school room floor. Along the wall was a bookcase filled with paperbacks except for the bottom shelf. The bottom shelf was filled with hard covered picture books.

"I like reading picture books," Mrs. Rief said defensively. The students' mouths hung open in shock. "Picture books are for everyone, not just elementary students," she continued.

This is what we'd soon come to know as a typical answer from Mrs. Rief. Over the course of the year we would become comfortable with her laid-back style of teaching. In her classroom students sat in groups of four around a table, instead of in rows of single desks. This allowed us to get help from our classmates for our writing instead of having to wait for a conference with the teacher. Writing about what we were interested in was something we were encouraged to do. With ten pages of writing due at the end of each week and class time allotted for writing, Mrs. Rief gave us a reason and time to write.

Unlike most classrooms, Mrs. Rief's room was as close to being a home as school could get. Plants filled the window sills, keeping the room from feeling like a jail. Posters covered the cement-block walls, lighting up the room with color. Students lounged around the edges of the room, using pads of paper as their desks.

At the beginning of the year the amount of reading we were expected to do almost every night seemed like torture, but by April we were begging for class reading time as well. Mrs. Rief had us keep reading logs in which we responded to what we had read. It was through these reading logs that we realized that reading and writing are connected. What we read influenced what we wrote. This is what Mrs. Rief wanted us to realize.

Sara's Story

In elementary school my favorite day of the week was Monday. Mondays were library days. The library was my favorite place in the school. It had warm red carpet, cushioned chairs, big sofas, plants, and thousands of books. I loved picture books, especially ones that were interesting and eye catching. My favorite books were the ones with colorful pictures and detailed drawings.

Picture books were an important part of my childhood. They allowed me to see actions and emotions that I could only imagine when I was reading or listening to books without pictures. They gripped me and brought me into the world of books. A world that felt too overpowering when I was so young. I know that if someone had handed me a hundred-page book with no pictures in first grade, I would have been discouraged, even afraid. Instead I was given books with words and pictures on every page. I was able to read what I saw, which fascinated me. I learned that many things can be explained in words and started to tackle longer, harder books.

I didn't really get back into picture books until I was given an open assignment by Mrs. Rief. We were told to research a topic of our choice. I chose to research an illustrator because I believed illustrators made me want to learn to read. As I looked through many children's books, I came across an illustrator who caught my attention, Trina Schart Hyman. The faces of the people in her drawings were incredibly expressive, and the borders around the text were as detailed as the pictures themselves.

Meanwhile, I also had a science project due. Fortunately, my teachers liked the idea of my integrating what I was learning in English class into a new project for science. I extended the research I did on Hyman to help me with my science project on marine science. We were given the choice of working alone or with a partner. My best friend, Jen and I decided that we would work together. We were given a long list of possible project ideas: poetry, watercolors, skits, lyrics, research projects, children's books, and so on. We thought a book would be a good idea. Jen liked to write, and I loved to draw, so we decided that if we combined our talents, we could come up with a children's book.

A children's book seemed like an easy, fun task, but we found out how much work and cooperation it takes. The first thing we had to decide was what we wanted to write about and what we wanted children to get out of it. We made a list of everything we had learned in the marine science unit. This list included animals like sea stars, sea urchins, peri-

FIGURE 6–1

winkles, crabs, jellyfish, sea gulls, and sand worms. The list also included facts, tips, and cautions about waves, tides, undertows, animals, and night time. From this list we took what we felt was the most important. We wanted the book to be educational and interesting. We chose things that we felt children would most likely see at the seashore and could relate to like the tide coming in and visiting grandparents. We felt a picture book was easier than a regular book because we didn't have to sound scientific. We would also be able to draw pictures to help say or get across what we wanted.

Before Jen wrote the story we discussed some ideas. I began to sketch characters, both a boy and a girl. (See Figure 6–1.) I felt that a boy would be better than a girl because I didn't like or feel comfortable with my drawings of the girl. We wanted this to be the first time Rick had been to the beach, so we decided that he should be visiting his grandparents. Jen wrote the first draft of the story, keeping in mind the things we had talked about. Together we went through it and corrected the mechanical

FIGURE 6–2

errors. I also told her where I felt the story should be changed. For example, I didn't think that I would be able to draw a recognizable jellyfish, so we substituted sea urchins. In another instance I knew that if I drew a crab on the rocks it would be hard to see him. I also felt that the boy would pick up the crab and put it in his bucket. We decided together the best solution would be to put the crab on the shovel and have the boy put it in the bucket. This change in the picture dictated a revision in the text. Originally Jen wrote, "Rick tries to pull at the mussels again, but a quick movement catches his eye. Rick turns to look just in time to see a small creature run under a rock. Turning the rock over, Rick finds a green crab." We decided to match the text more closely with the picture I'd make and added, "Taking his shovel, Rick picks up the crab, fills his bucket with water, and puts the crab in it." (See Figure 6–2.)

After completing the story together, we worked on choosing a title. We made a list of possible titles and from that list we chose *Exploring with Rick*. We wanted it to make the reader wonder. By entitling the story *Exploring with Rick*, we thought children would want to know what Rick was exploring.

The next step was to break the story up into sections or pages. We wanted each page to cover a certain scene or topic. For example, the first page of text set the scene. The second page tells about seaweed and periwinkles. (See Figure 6–3.) We decided there should be an illustration for each page of text. Together we decided what I should draw. We discussed different possibilities for the scenes and any difficulties I thought I might have. For instance, I didn't feel that I would be able to draw the front of the boy, so for the cover and ending page, I drew the boy walking away. (See Figure 6–4.) That way I was able to draw the back of the boy and feel comfortable about my drawing. I felt that the pages with text were

FIGURE 6–3

FIGURE 6–4

going to be boring and thought we should add more color. I showed Jen some of Hyman's work and the borders she drew around the text. We thought that would make our book more colorful, exciting, and eye catching for the reader. I designed the borders and drew them. Together Jen and I colored the borders, making each kind of seaweed and shell the same color throughout all the pages, which integrated our science knowledge. (See Figure 6–5.) When I was finished drawing and coloring all the illustrations, Jen and I covered each page with contact paper and assembled the book.

Working together on the book made the task seem much easier. We were able to combine ideas and discuss possibilities. Each of us grew up differently and each had different feelings about the beach. I always went to the beach when I was at my grandparents. Jen looked for crabs in the

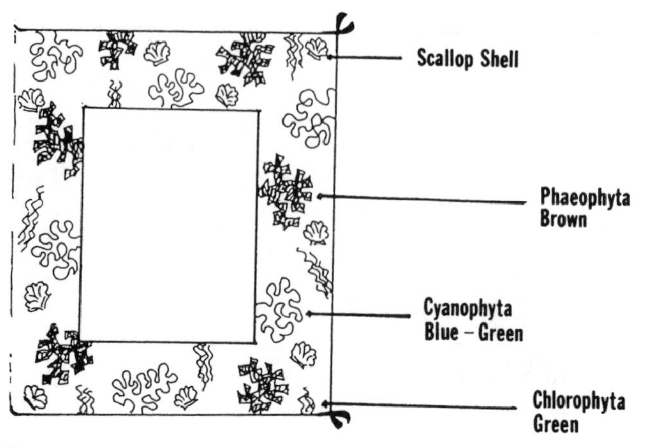

FIGURE 6–5

rocks with her brothers when she went to the beach. By working together, we were able to combine our feelings about the seashore and come up with a book for all children.

I can imagine a child walking into the library, picking up *Exploring with Rick*, looking at it, and saying, "I want to read this book." He or she would sit down on the carpet or in a cushioned chair and would flip through the pages thinking, "I can read this book." I would have the privilege of knowing that I helped a child enter the world of books.

Tricia's Story

> Words we hear create images in our minds. Pictures are visual words.

The moon stares out over the landscape from behind a mountain. Except for the hardy grasses and sharp rocks, the earth stretches out in all directions, flat and empty. From her lookout, mother moon lights a path for her son, the coyote. The night is black, gray, and white, the colors of the day stolen away with the sun. Outside mother moon's protecting light it's dark and shadowy. From out of this darkness anything might jump. But all that follows coyote is his shadow, stretched out long and silent behind him. It's nothing short of torture to have his mother moon so close but never quite within reach. His shadow offers him no consolation or explanation of what he's done to deserve such isolation. My words create a picture, just as Ronald Himler's pictures brought these words to my mind.

In March Mrs. Rief announced a long-term assignment due at the end of the year. We had to research any topic using three types of writing, then present what we'd learned in three different genres. From the smile on her face we could see she had visions of poems, essays, letters, and children's books. I was angry. "Just what I need," I thought. We already had science and social studies projects due at that same time. It wasn't even the type of project you could put off until the night before it was due and whip something off. The next day we were expected to have an idea for a topic. At dinner I talked with my Mom about it.

"How about an author you like or a hobby," she suggested.

"No, that's boring," I grumbled.

"Then how about Arizona? You're going there this summer."

It might be interesting, I thought, but somehow it wasn't quite what I wanted. I decided to put off making a decision until later. The next day in class there was a pile of books on the table; I still didn't have a topic so to make it look like I was doing some work I picked up *I'm in Charge of Celebrations* by Byrd Baylor.

Behind a web of branches and small desert brush, a coyote stops in his tracks, alert but not scared. He stands atop a barren slope, shaded in browns and golds. A girl with long black hair, dressed in the colors of the sand, stops her ascent toward the coyote. Her height dwarfs the nearby cactuses. The sun slips behind the hill, its last warm rays fall upon the tracks of wild animals mixed with the barefoot prints of the girl. Strange magic fills the air like smoke as the coyote and girl stare without fear into each others' eyes.

I decided my project would be to find out about the beliefs and folklore of the Native Americans of the western states. *I'm in Charge of Celebrations* and other books I found like it were what convinced me. The words and feelings the pictures created made the characters and their messages in the writing come to life. Mrs. Rief brought in all the books she had at home that she thought might help. At first I read novels, *Sing Down the Moon* and *Stream to the River, River to the Sea*. The latter book showed me that Indians have a very clear understanding of their identity, of who they are. With each book I read I made notes in my reading log, copying down lines I liked and important ideas, so I'd be able to remember the things I'd noticed when it came time to do the writing. Together these books gave me an idea of what day-to-day life was like for the Indian, but the story lines seemed to get in the way of the culture I was trying to discover.

So I read *Dancing Teepees*, a picture book of poems by Native Americans. Around each poem there was a border, some were of woven blankets, and others were pictures of the heavens with stars as full of life and warmth as a racing heart. Paintings of figures that the Indians had scratched into a rock bordered another page. There were beetles, sheep, birds, and men all the same size, all of equal importance. Every word in each poem had been carefully chosen, making the poems straight to the point. The authors used language carefully; by not using extra words they show it respect. Some of the poems were translations of traditional ceremonies like the Omaha ceremony for the newborn or the Paiute cradle song.

The poems were written about what the Native Americans cared most deeply for. That's what poetry is: the expression of feelings that go beyond everyday language. After reading *Dancing Teepees*, I stopped reading the novels and looked for more picture books.

Usually, when I've had to do projects for school, there have been certain books I've turned to, encyclopedias for facts, atlases for statistics, and novels for book reports. But I'd never before thought of using picture books. I had a preconceived idea that all picture books are written simplistically: "Little Jimmy went to the store. He bought some bread and milk. On the way home a big dog barked at him." I thought of them as bedtime stories or the first books children can read to themselves. But I discovered that's not how all of them are written. If children's books are written well, they're for everyone, and I'll never outgrow them.

I read another book by Byrd Baylor, *The Desert Is Theirs*. Boulders fill the path that the women walk along. Their footsteps form a trail of red indentations in the hot desert sand. Only where the rocks toss their shade do the desert grasses grow. But above all the sweat and heat of the ground soars the hawk, like a spirit of the icy blue. For him the air is cool and the heat of the sun affects him only as it creates the thermals he floats upon. He is the one made for this place, he belongs; the people bow their heads in respect to him when he passes.

It's impossible to say what I got from each book. My notes for *Dancing Teepees* are short: "The spoken word was sacred. Passed on stories and memories through it. Respected elders." Most of the books left me with a feeling, but nothing I was able to take notes on. I can only describe it as an understanding, as close as I could come to knowing the Native Americans without ever having met them.

These picture books can teach the reader more in thirty-two pages, through their pictures and words, than many books do in three hundred pages. For example, they taught me things about our relationship to the earth and each other. The books show the Indians' dependence on and respect for the earth. They are poetic, getting across their message without being dreary, burdensome, or boring. The more I read the more jealous I became of the Native American's closeness to the earth.

The night before the final project was due I was looking through what I had written and realized I still needed one more piece of writing. According to the clock, it was already 11:00 P.M. I grabbed a piece of paper and started to write. Everything I'd seen in the books: speech patterns, ideas, images, it all came together as I wrote "Benediction." In the morning I handed it in, not wanting to make revisions.

Benediction

The weariness in my body pushes me to sleep, but my
heart is thinking many thoughts.

Indians are one soul, we learn through the old who
have known the soul of the earth the longest.

The earth has the oldest soul of all.

My inside self sings loudly when the ground is
decorated with water bringing it life.

It's often hard to hold it inside so I don't show how
happy I am.

But by the fire-side you can see my soul dance with
happiness in the shadows.

I'm happiest though when the sun sets the cliffs on
fire and warms the stones from the cold of night.

The sheep laugh as they walk up the path.

The land is clean and wonderful.

My soul answers the earth's soul when it speaks like
this, hoping for praise.

We talk without a human word.

But we say "I am Indian, my veins pump with the same
red clay of the hills. My baby sleeps the quiet sleep
of the mountains and becomes strong. The land is my
friend. Without her I die."

We've been given our eyes to see and react to life, and words to pass what we've seen on to others. Picture books are able to combine both of these. When we're little, we like books for the pictures of animals and the stories. But when we get older, we can find more meaning in the words. The pictures don't just visualize what the words are saying, instead they go beyond the words giving clues to the depths of meaning in the words. These picture books can never be outgrown.

Works Cited

O'Dell, Scott. 1980. *Sing Down the Moon*. New York: Random House.

———. 1986. *Stream to the River, River to the Sea*. Boston: Houghton Mifflin.

7

Good Children's Literature Is For Everyone, ~~Even~~ Especially Adolescents

Linda Rief

When the argument broke out in my eighth-grade class, it wasn't about Julie breaking up with Matt. It wasn't about Jeff picking on Devin. It wasn't about detention rules, or unrealistic homework assignments, or the insufficient number of school dances, or who had the carpet last during reading time. It was about Winnie-the-Pooh—specifically, Tigger.

"I like A. A. Milne," Jamie said, "because he writes simply. As a kid I could relate to all the characters. They're all good. Except for Tigger. He's mean."

"What?" Josh asked, looking up from his writing. "Tigger is NOT mean. He's just a happy-go-lucky kind'a guy."

Ben joined Jamie. "He is *too* mean. He bounces Eeyore all the time. He wrecks Rabbit's garden. He. . . . "

"Tigger just tries to humor Eeyore," responded Josh. "It's all a joke, in fun. He tries to give Eeyore a greater sense of appeal, but Eeyore never accepts it. Eeyore takes life too seriously. He can't take a joke."

"It's not a joke," Jamie said. "Served Tigger right when his stripes came off the time they washed him."

"Didn't bother him a bit," said Josh.

Angie and Kate snickered and giggled through the entire argument. *Jamie* and *Josh* seriously arguing about a character from *Winnie-the-Pooh*?

Jamie loves the outdoors. He rows every morning on the river for a local crew team in a two man skull. He reads Patrick McManus, who writes adult books (*They Shoot Canoes, Don't They?*, *Never Sniff a Gift Fish*, etc.), voraciously.

Josh is a latent hippie. He wears tie-dyed shirts, peace-sign necklaces, wrists full of leather-woven bracelets, and often a bandanna. He is obsessed with Jim Morrison (lead singer for *The Doors*), reading everything he can, written about, or by, the deceased lyricist/singer. Josh has notebooks filled with his own poetry, highly influenced by Morrison's own writing.

To hear Jamie and Josh arguing about Tigger surprised me too. It shouldn't. I know good children's literature, including picture books, is for everyone. I've tried to ensure that my classroom is filled with it. I intentionally share children's literature as part of everything we do. And yet, at times, I forget how much children's literature sticks with our adolescents, and should be a part of their lives.

The argument between Jamie and Josh had arisen while I was talking with Jamie about his upcoming class presentation about an author. I was simply confirming the author he had chosen and letting him know his due date. Out of curiosity I asked him, "What made you choose Milne?"

> I like all the styles in his books. There are songs, poems, stories, games, dialogue. . . . Sometimes Winnie-the-Pooh even hums to himself. . . . Some of the sentences are three words long, some are twenty words. I like that. He does things and thinks the way kids understand him. When my friend Chris and I were little we'd play some of the games he did. Pooh gets pine cones, and he and Piglet race them down the river. We'd do the same thing. We'd put sticks in them and make boats out of them. We'd race to a bridge and see whose boat reached it first.
>
> Pictures are important too. I could carry in my mind what the characters looked like. Even though they're animals they come to life and have problems that I could relate to. Like Pooh. He looks out for all the other characters. He knows when they feel bad. Piglet got stuck one time. Pooh knew he was in trouble and rescued him from a flood. He remembers Piglet's and Eeyore's birthdays when no one else remembers. Pooh is the kindest of all the characters.
>
> Rabbit is conceited. Owl thinks he's the smartest, but he messes up a lot. Piglet feels sorry for himself because he's so small and Kanga gets all the attention. Eeyore is a wanderer. He doesn't notice a lot because no one notices him.

> I've read every A. A. Milne book. They're like Robert Fulghum's *All I Really Need to Know I Learned in Kindergarten* [1988]. I like Milne because his books are written simply. As a kid I could relate to all the characters. They are all good. Except Tigger. He's mean. . . .

I had no idea Jamie or Josh knew, or cared, so much about Winnie-the-Pooh. The conversation confirmed for me the need to continue to surround my students with the finest literature, including children's literature and picture books.

Children's picture books are not only enjoyed and appreciated by older students, but they have an intrinsic appeal. "Look at *Where the Wild Things Are* (Sendak, 1963) if you wonder why picture books appeal to adolescents," notes Tom Newkirk. "Max is bad. He's the 'baddest' of all the wild things. He's made king of the wild things and he *still* gets his supper." (Newkirk, 1991)

I do several things to keep adolescents in touch with this literature.

I Fill the Classroom with Children's Literature and Picture Books, Those That Contain the Richest Language and the Finest Illustrations

I collect children's picture books. The students know I value them because the room is filled with them. If they are mixed with all the other genres there is no mistaking children's books as baby books.

Good children's literature is for everyone, not just young children. The language is often poetic, filled with metaphor, and crisp in its simplicity. The illustrations are fine examples of the best art: watercolors, pen and ink drawings, wood cuts, oils and other mediums. I look for artists like Chris Van Allsburg, Trina Schart Hyman, Jan Brett, Steven Kellogg, Paul Goble, Peter Parnall, David Macaulay, Ted Rand, Julie Vivas, David Weisner, Don Wood, Susan Jeffers, Tom Feelings, and Stephen Gammel.

Reference books and recommendations from colleagues, friends and students are helpful in finding good picture books. Finding a bookstore, however, that specializes in children's literature is most helpful. I find the best books by looking through the shelves and taking time on the spot to read through them. That way, I find the literature I love. (See the bibliography at the end of this chapter.)

I Read Children's Literature and Picture Books Aloud

Like fine poetry, children's picture books are meant to be seen and heard. Even adolescents like to be read to. The books are language rich. For the most part we just enjoy the story, the words, and the illustrations. At times, we talk specifically about message, about character, about language, about pictures, about literary devices, about issues, . . .

Because these books are short, they are wonderful to read to begin or end a class. By reading aloud I not only let kids hear the richness of the language, but I invite adolescents to read them also. If I'm reading them, they realize it's okay for them to read them. By leaving them around the room, all the kids know they are invited to pick them up. While the language and artwork often challenges the proficient readers, the clarity and simplicity allows the weaker readers access to fine books, and complicated issues. I would rather a student, who has limited reading ability, pick up Jane Yolen's *Owl Moon* than a high-interest-low level reader that *interests* no one and is filled with empty words.

I Use Children's Literature and Picture Books Along with Any Themes Being Studied

No matter what the theme or topic (generations, prejudice, war, the environment, animals, Native Americans etc.) I try to collect and use picture books that relate to the subject. In the book *Seeking Diversity* (Rief, 1991), there are lists of picture books that I use most often in the middle grades. If we are studying war, I read *Rose Blanche* (Innocenti, 1985), *Hiroshima No Pika* (Maruki, 1980), and *Faithful Elephants* (Tsuchiya, 1988). If we are researching environmental issues, I include *The Great Kapok Tree* (Cherry, 1990) *Just a Dream* (Van Allsburg, 1990), and *Moon Song* (Baylor, 1982). If students are writing about generations, I hand them *Wilfred Gordon McDonald Partridge* (Fox, 1985), *How Does It Feel to Be Old?* (Farber, 1979), and *Emma* (Kesselman, 1980).

I Encourage Sharing Books That Include Children's Authors and Illustrators

I share authors and books frequently with my students. This sharing intentionally includes children's authors and illustrators. Each student (I have five classes of approximately twenty-five students each) is responsible for sharing information about one author for a week. They may do it alone or work with partners. They have five minutes at the beginning of each class period during their week to read an excerpt they find especially effective from their author's writing. If they have chosen picture-book authors, they often share whole books. I encourage a diversity of books by the same author. On Friday, they have ten minutes to teach us the most unique information they found out or discovered about their author or the author's writing. They may use any format for the presentation. They know my goals are to introduce other students to a variety of authors, to let them hear fine writing, and to let students study best-liked authors in depth.

Jan Brett is one of my favorite illustrators. On Monday I read *The First Dog*, on Tuesday *Annie and the Wild Animals*, Wednesday *The Mitten*, and Thursday *The Wild Christmas Reindeer*. Each day I ask the students to respond in their logs to what they noticed about Brett's texts or illustrations. On Friday we discuss their observations, and I share what I've found out about Brett and her writing.

Like Jamie, who chose A. A. Milne as his author, other students choose children's authors also. Krista chose Dr. Seuss; Marcos chose Astrid Lindgren; Alisha, Maurice Sendak. It is not an accident that these students choose children's authors. They know I value these authors as much as I value the authors of adult novels or adolescent fiction because I read and share all of these genres too. They are invited to share their favorite picture book authors and illustrators.

I Use Storytelling of Children's Books, as a Way into Owning a Good Story. I read a variety of folktales, fairy tales, myths, legends, and epic poems from picture books to the students. I add many contemporary stories and adaptations of the same genre to piles of books I stack on each desk, and ask the students to find a story they like. I show them how to tell a story using their voices and facial expressions. They learn the stories they choose, and present them as a storytelling, or story theater. Some students do it individually and become all the characters. Other students audition parts and tell the story together.

Kalim, using a guitar, told and sang *The Jolly Mon* by Jimmy Buffet. Drew auditioned parts for William Steig's *Shrek*. Six students took on other characters and backed Drew up as he narrated the story and spoke the part of Shrek. Olivia found three students to tell *The Dancing Skeleton*, complete with Jen on the fiddle. Elementary students love the storytelling. My students learn how to use voice and facial expressions, and how to engage an audience, along with learning how to tell a good story.

They learn other things as well. "*Jolly Mon* wasn't really a children's book," said Kalim. "You could read it to a child, but an adult would enjoy it too. The illustrations were very realistic."

"I liked being in front of the class telling the story because it made me nervous, and for me to do it and do it good, was a nice feeling," said Steve.

"I could create the voices and see the people in my mind," added Kyle. "The pictures were like guidelines. All I had to do was put them in motion."

"I had fun," said Drew. "[The storytelling] was like acting for me. I became Shrek. I *was* ugly. . . . It was fun to hear other people read and remember the stories I read as a kid. I like to have pictures in my reading or listen to literature. It helps me get an idea. . . . It was also nice just to hear the voices of the stories in my head, like *Knots on a Counting Rope* [Bill Martin]."

"Children's picture books aren't as easy as they seem to be. They aren't simple. *Knots on a Counting Rope* doesn't have hard words, but it has a grownup idea to it," noted Tara.

"I liked how everybody really got into the stories," said Steve. "As they told them it was like they were the characters. . . . I think things always go better when they're fun. This was fun."

I Encourage Reading, Writing, and Illustrating in the Children's Literature and Picture Book Genre, Throughout the Year

I ask the students to consider trying children's picture books as readers, writers, and illustrators. I allow them to collaborate with each other. I make sure there are plenty of models around the room so they can see how professional authors and illustrators do it. I encourage them to create their own collaborative pieces as they study balances between texts and illustrations.

Illustrations are as important as words. Barbara Cooney, well-known author/illustrator, described the relationship as being like a string of pearls, where the text is the string and the illustrations are the pearls. "The text comes first," Cooney said, "then I wrap my illustrations around it" (1990).

Chris and Tye chose to write a children's story after researching animals and children's books for more than six weeks. This was Tye's first year out of the resource room for English class. In light of Tye's prior experience with learning problems, their book and dedication ("Dedicated to all children who can't get out of their shell.") takes on added meaning. (See Figure 7–1, which shows part of their book.)

Jen wrote, while Sara illustrated, *First in the Family*, a story about the negative aspects, and eventual positives, of growing up the oldest in a large family. (See Figure 7–2 for part of the story.) Sara worked hard at coordinating her pictures with Jen's words. It is evident they both enjoyed playing with language.

Tricia used many of Byrd Baylor's books as she studied Native Americans (See Chapter 6). She didn't write a children's book. She learned *from* children's books.

After seeing the movie *Dances with Wolves*, Katie became very interested in Native Americans. She attended a festival at Dartmouth College, read picture books, poetry anthologies and novels, and interviewed Native Americans. One of the ways she chose to present her findings was through a picture book. She wrote the text and asked Brian to draw the illustrations. She did the borders around pages. (See Figure 7–3.)

FIGURE 7–1: *From Chris and Tye's Book*

Katie embeds several issues in her text. Only boys are allowed to hunt and must spend the night in the woods to prove their manhood. The chief's daughter, Running Deer, asks for the same opportunity. "Father, I know that this manhood journey is only supposed to be for boys but I am as strong or stronger than some of the boys. I can run faster than most of them too. Can I please have the chance to prove to myself and to this whole tribe by taking the journey myself?"

Little Bear and his friends are angry and "muttered and protested to themselves, but no one dared say anything because Running Deer was the Chief's daughter . . . They figured also that the Chief was putting Running

FIGURE 7–2: *From* First in the Family

Deer's journey on the same night as Little Bear's, because if something happened Little Bear would be there to help."

In the story Little Bear wastes time finding a spot, ends up sleeping in an ill-chosen cave (with a very angry bear), and needs rescuing– by Running Deer. So as not to "humiliate" Little Bear, Running Deer offers him her cave for the night. When they return in the morning, Little Bear tells the truth. Running Deer is allowed to hunt, even though she's a girl. "Then the Chief announced that even though Running Deer helped Little Bear, he showed his manhood by telling the truth . . . and he was permitted to hunt also."

FIGURE 7–3: A *Spread from Katie's Story*

Mark and Jim created a children's story entitled "Liver!" The illustrations are so descriptive they can almost stand on their own. (See Figure 7–4.)

Drew and Barry had a wonderful time creating a picture book "for the sophisticated reader" (in their words) about the last dinosaur (See Figure 7–5). An excerpt reads:

> Platty was feeling pretty swell. He slipped into his monogrammed robe, stretched, yawned, and looked skyward. THAT was the biggest mistake of the dinosaur's puny, insignificant, worthless life.
>
> . . . Platty believed the object hurling down on him to be a fastball pitched by God in an interstellar game of baseball. This was an incorrect assumption. Although he analyzed the object's speed correctly at Mach 38, he had made a slight miscalculation in estimating the size. The "ball" was a tad larger than assumed (about the size of Sri Lanka), and besides, there weren't any outfielders. Platty, still working under the incorrect assumption, picked up his Louisville Slugger 1 (This is a footnote. Please look under footnote at this time. Thank you.) and his batting helmet . . .
>
> *Footnote* 1: *A Brief History of Louisville Sluggers*
>
> Back in Platty's time when baseball first began, there were no bats. Instead, players used real slugs. This is why some bats

FIGURE 7–4: *Illustration from* Liver!

> still carry the name slugger. Louisville is the place where these slugs were found, which is why it, too, is on bats to date.

I want Drew and Barry, Mark and Jim, Sara and Jen—to learn to work with each other. I want them to play with language and play with pictures.

I want my classroom to be a laboratory for the language arts, not just the written word. I don't want what happened to Trina Schart Hyman to happen to Sara (See Chapter 6).

Hyman, one of America's finest children's illustrators, was never allowed to draw in school.

> I couldn't ever concentrate on what I was supposed to be learning about, because all I wanted to do was to be left alone,

FIGURE 7–5: *From Drew and Barry's Book*

FIGURE 7–6: *From Sara and Jen's Story*

> to read books, or listen to music, or to draw pictures of witches and princesses when I should have been learning fractions. After eleven years, I came out of the public school system believing I was a hopelessly stupid little creature who would never be able to learn or to think (1981).

I Encourage the Study, Reading, and Writing of Children's Literature Across the Disciplines

In *Coming to Know* (Atwell, 1990), Donna Maxim has put together a succinct chapter and a lengthy appendix that lists children's books for content area study. Although she is in a third-grade classroom, I find I use many of the same books in the seventh and eighth grade.

FIGURE 7–7: *Dick and Jane Visit the Massachusetts Bay Colony*

For example, Sara's illustrations of Jen's text for their final science project are rich lessons from Trina Schart Hyman and Jan Brett. The ornate borders show what Sara learned from tidal pools along the seacoast during the study of marine biology. Brett uses borders to tell all the details she can't fit into the main story. Sara used borders to show all the marine life she and Jen discovered in these field trips, among them sea anemones, limpids, urchins, sponges, mussels, algae. (Figure 7–6 shows part of their story. See other illustrations from this book in Chapter 6.)

While Sara and Jen created a children's book in response to their studies of marine biology in Lee Andrews' science class, Sandy designed her own response to a social studies assignment. She played with language after reading *More Fun with Dick and Jane*, as she sketched and wrote a book entitled *Dick and Jane Visit the Massachusetts Bay Colony*. (See Figure 7–7.)

I want the students to take children's picture books beyond the classroom, both figuratively and literally, both now and later in their lives, carried in their hands, and in their heads. Chandolyne did. "Can I borrow this book to read to my little sister?" she asked, holding *Make Way for Ducklings* by Robert McCloskey. Two weeks later she still had it out. "I can't help it," she said. "My little sister wants me to read it to her every night."

I want students like Jamie and Josh to surprise me over arguments about Tigger. The surprises tell me there's a lot of thinking that goes on in our classrooms that we never know about. There's a lot that happens by inviting ~~even~~ especially adolescents into children's picture books. We're never aware of most of that thinking. It all counts.

Works Cited:

Atwell, Nancie, (ed.). 1990. *Coming to Know*. Portsmouth, NH: Heinemann.

Baylor, Byrd. 1982. Illustrated by Ronald Himler. New York: Scribner's.

Cherry, Lynne. 1990. *The Great Kapok Tree*. San Diego, CA: Gulliver Books.

Cooney, Barbara. July 17, 1990. Address at the University of New Hampshire.

Farber, Norma. Illustrated by Trina Schart Hyman. 1979. *How Does It Feel To Be Old?*. New York: E.P. Dutton.

Fox, Mem. Illustrated by Julie Vivas. 1985. *Wilfred Gordon McDonald Partridge*. New York: Viking Penguin.

Fulghum, Robert. 1988. *All I Really Need to Know I Learned in Kindergarten*. New York: Villard Books.

Gallant, Marc Gregory. 1986. *More Fun with Dick and Jane*. New York: Penguin.

Hyman, Trina Schart. 1981. *Self-Portrait: Trina Schart Hyman*. Reading, MA: Addison-Wesley.

Innocenti, Roberto. 1985. *Rose Blanche*. Minnesota: Creative Education.

Maruki, Toshi. 1980. *Hiroshima No Pika*. New York: Lothrop, Lee and Shepard.

McCloskey, Robert. 1969. *Make Way for Ducklings*. New York: Viking.
McManus, Patrick F. 1982. *They Shoot Canoes, Don't They?* New York: Henry Holt.
McManus, Patrick F. 1984. *Never Sniff a Gift Fish*. New York: Henry Holt.
Morimoto, Junko. 1987. *My Hiroshima*. New York: Viking Penguin.
Newkirk, Thomas. November, 1991. Presentation at NCTE. Seattle, WA.
Rief, Linda. 1992. *Seeking Diversity*. Portsmouth, NH: Heinemann.
Tsuchiya, Yukio. Illustrated by Ted Lewin. 1988. *Faithful Elephants*. Boston: Houghton Mifflin.
Van Allsburg, Chris. 1990. *Just a Dream*. Boston, MA: Houghton Mifflin.
Yolen, Jane, Illustrated by John Schoenherr. 1987. *Owl Moon*. New York: Putnam.

PICTURE BOOKS *that focus on the creative process*

Bjork, Christina and Anderson, Lena. 1987. *Linnea in Monet's Garden*. New York: Farrar, Straus and Giroux. (Linnea, a little girl, visits the painter Claude Monet's garden and sees many of his famous paintings in Paris.)

Collins, Judy. Illustrated by Jane Dyer. 1989. *My Father*. Boston: Little, Brown and Company. (A shared dream carries family members out of their drab life into a finer world of music and travel, a dream later fulfilled by the youngest daughter when she becomes a parent herself.)

De Paola, Tomie. 1989. *The Art Lesson*. New York: G.P. Putnam's Sons. (Having learned to be creative in drawing pictures at home, young Tommy is dismayed when he goes to school and finds the art lesson there much more regimented.)

Fleischman, Paul. Illustrated by Janet Wentworth. 1988. *Rondo in C*. New York: Harper and Row. (As a young piano student plays Beethoven's Rondo in C at her recital, each member of the audience is stirred by memories.)

Kesselman, Wendy. Illustrated by Barbara Cooney. 1980. *Emma*. New York: Doubleday. (Motivated by a birthday gift, a 72-year-old woman begins to paint.)

Lionni, Leo. 1967. *Frederick*. New York: Alfred A. Knopf. (While his relatives gather food and seek shelter, a small mouse gathers images and dreams to sustain his family through the long winter.)

Reading is Fundamental. 1986. *Once Upon a Time*. New York: G.P. Putnam's Sons. (Illustrated collection of true and fictional anecdotes and stories by well-known children's authors and illustrators about reading.)

Rylant, Cynthia. Illustrated by Peter Catalanotto. 1988. *All I See*. New York: Orchard Books. (A child paints with an artist friend who sees and paints only whales.)

Exceptional Illustrators *and some of their finest works (authors in parentheses)*

Aliki

A Medieval Feast. 1983. New York: Harper Trophy.

Mummies Made in Egypt. 1979. New York: Harper Trophy.

The Two of Them. 1979. New York: Greenwillow Books.

Graeme Base

Jabberwocky (Lewis Carroll). 1989. New York: Harry N. Abrams.

My Grandma Lived in Gooligulch. 1988. CA: The Australian Book Source.

The Eleventh Hour. 1988. New York: Viking Kestrel.

Jan Brett

The Mitten. 1989. New York: G.P. Putnam's Sons.

Beauty and the Beast. 1989. New York: Clarion Books.

The First Dog. 1988. San Diego: Harcourt Brace Jovanovich.

Goldilocks and the Three Bears. 1987. New York: Dodd, Mead and Co.

Annie and the Wild Animals. 1985. Boston: Houghton Mifflin.

Fritz and the Beautiful Horses. 1981. Boston: Houghton Mifflin.

The Wild Christmas Reindeer. 1990. New York: G.P. Putnam's Sons.

Marcia Brown

Shadow (from the French of Blaise Cendrars). 1982. New York: Charles Scribner's Sons.

Barbara Cooney

Louhi. Witch of North Farm (Toni de Gerez). 1986. New York: Viking Kestrel.

Miss Rumphius. 1985. New York: Viking Penguin.

Ox-cart Man (Donald Hall). 1979. New York: Viking Kestrel.

Hattie and the Wild Waves. 1990. New York: Viking.

Tomie de Paola

The Mountains of Quilt (Nancy Willard). 1987. San Diego: Harcourt Brace Jovanovich.

The Quilt Story (Tony Johnston). 1985. New York: G.P. Putnam's Sons.

The Legend of the Blue Bonnet. 1983. New York: G.P. Putnam's Sons.

Now One Foot, Now the Other. 1981. New York: G.P. Putnam's Sons.

The Kids' Cat Book. 1979. New York: Holiday House.

Nana Upstairs and Nana Downstairs. 1973. New York: G.P. Putnam's Sons.

Tom Feelings

Now Sheba Sings the Song (Maya Angelou). 1987. New York: E.P. Dutton.

Daydreamers (Eloise Greenfield). 1981. New York: Dial Books.

Something on my Mind (Nikki Grimes). 1978. New York: Dial Books.
jambo means hello (Muriel Feelings). 1974. New York: Dial Books.

Stephen Gammell

Dancing Teepees (Poems selected by Virginia Driving Hawk Sneve). 1989. New York: Holiday House.
Airmail to the Moon (Tom Birdseye). 1988. New York: Holiday House.
Song and Dance Man (Karen Ackerman). 1988. New York: Alfred A. Knopf.
Old Henry (Joan Blos). 1987. New York: William Morrow.
Waiting to Waltz—A Childhood (Poems by Cynthia Rylant). 1984. New York: Bradbury Press.

T.S. Geisel (Dr. Seuss)

You're Only Old Once!. 1986. New York: Random House.
The Butter Battle Book. 1984. New York: Random House.

Paul Goble:

Beyond the Ridge. 1989. New York: Bradbury Press.
Death of the Iron Horse. 1987. New York: Bradbury Press.
Buffalo Woman. 1984. New York: Bradbury Press.

Trina Schart Hyman

Swan Lake (Told by Margot Fonteyn). 1989. San Diego: Gulliver Books.
Canterbury Tales (Selected, translated and adapted by Barbara Cohen). 1988. New York: Lothrop, Lee and Shepard Books.
St. George and the Dragon (Retold by Margaret Hodges). 1984. Boston: Little, Brown and Co.
Little Red Riding Hood. 1983. New York: Holiday House.
How Does It Feel to Be Old? (Norma Farber). 1979. New York: E.P. Dutton.
The Sleeping Beauty. 1977. Boston: Little, Brown and Co.
Snow White (Translated from the German by Paul Heins). 1974. Boston: Little, Brown and Co.

Susan Jeffers

Hiawatha (Henry Wadsworth Longfellow). 1983. New York: Dial Books.
Stopping by Woods on a Snowy Evening (Robert Frost). 1978. New York: E.P. Dutton.

Steven Kellogg

Is Your Mama a Llama? (Deborah Guarino). 1989. New York: Scholastic.
Johnny Appleseed. 1988. New York: William Morrow and Co.

Best Friends. 1986. New York: E.P. Dutton.
Pecos Bill. 1986. New York: William Morrow and Co.
The Island of the Skog. 1973. New York: Dial Books.

David Macaulay
Castle. 1977. Boston: Houghton Mifflin.
Pyramid. 1975. Boston: Houghton Mifflin.
Cathedral. 1973. Boston: Houghton Mifflin.

James Marshall
Goldilocks and the Three Bears. 1988. New York: Dial Books.
Red Riding Hood. 1987. New York: Dial Books.

Wendell Minor
Heartland (Diane Siebert). 1989. New York: Thomas Y. Crowell.
Mojave (Diane Siebert). 1988. New York: Thomas Y. Crowell.

Peter Parnall
Quiet. 1989. New York: Morrow Junior Books.
Feet. 1988. New York: Macmillan.
Apple Tree. 1987. New York: Macmillan.
Desert Voices (Byrd Baylor). 1981. New York: Charles Scribner's Sons.
The Other Way to Listen (Byrd Baylor). 1978. New York: Charles Scribner's Sons.
Woodpile. 1990. New York: Macmillan.
Cats From Away. 1989. New York: Macmillan.

Ted Rand
Once When I Was Scared (Helene Clare Pittman). 1988. New York: E.P. Dutton.
Knots on a Counting Rope (Bill Martin Jr. and John Archambault). 1987. New York: Henry Holt.
Barn Dance! (Bill Martin Jr. and John Archambault). 1986. New York: Henry Holt.
The Ghost-Eye Tree (Bill Martin Jr. and John Archambault). 1985. New York: Holt, Rinehart and Winston.

Chris Van Allsburg
Swan Lake (Mark Helprin). 1989. Boston: Ariel Books.
Two Bad Ants. 1988. Boston: Houghton Mifflin.
The Polar Express. 1985. Boston: Houghton Mifflin.
The Wreck of the Zephyr. 1983. Boston: Houghton Mifflin.
Jumanji. 1981. Boston: Houghton Mifflin.

Julie Vivas
The Nativity. 1986. San Diego: Gulliver Books.

Wilfred Gordon MacDonald Partridge (Mem Fox). 1984. New York: Viking Kestrel.

Possum Magic (Mem Fox). 1983. Tennessee: Abingdon Press.

The Very Best of Friends (Margaret Wild). 1989. New York: HBJ.

David Weisner

Free Fall. 1988. New York: Lothrop, Lee and Shepard.

Kite Flier (Dennis Haseley). 1986. New York: Four Winds Press.

Don Wood

Heckedy Peg (Audrey Wood). 1987. San Diego: Harcourt Brace Jovanovich.

King Bidgood's in the Bathtub (Audrey Wood). 1985. San Diego: Harcourt Brace Jovanovich.

The Napping House (Audrey Wood). 1984. San Diego: Harcourt Brace Jovanovich.

Moon Flute (Audrey Wood). 1980. San Diego: Harcourt Brace Jovanovich.

STORYTELLING:

Bang, Molly Garrett. 1976. *Wiley and the Hairy Man*. New York: Aladdin Books.

Buffett, Jimmy and Savannah Jane. Illustrated by Lambert Davis. 1988. *The Jolly Mon*. New York: HBJ.

DeFelice, Cynthia C. Illustrated by Robert Andrew Parker. 1989. *The Dancing Skeleton*. New York: Macmillan.

Galdone, Joanna. Illustrated by Paul Galdone. 1977. *The Tailypo*. New York: Clarion Books.

de Gerez, Toni. Illustrated by Barbara Cooney. 1986. *Louhi, Witch of North Farm*. New York: Viking Kestrel.

Grifalconi, Ann. 1986. *The Village of Round and Square Houses*. Boston: Little, Brown and Company.

Mahy, Margaret. Illustrated by Jean and Mou-sien Tseng. 1990. *The Seven Chinese Brothers*. New York: Scholastic.

Martin, Bill Jr. and Archambault, John. Illustrated by Ted Rand. 1985. *The Ghost-Eye Tree*. New York: Henry Holt.

Martin, Bill Jr. and Archambault, John. Illustrated by Ted Rand. 1987. *Knots on a Counting Rope*. New York: Henry Holt.

McKissack, Patricia C. Illustrated by Rachel Isadora. 1986. *Flossie and the Fox*. New York: Dial.

McKissack, Patricia C. Illustrated by Jerry Pinkney. 1988. *Mirandy and Brother Wind*. New York: Alfred A. Knopf.

Munsch, Robert and Kusugak, Michael. Illustrated by Vladyana Krykorka. 1988. *A Promise is a Promise*. Ontario: Annick Press.

Rappaport, Doreen. Illustrated by Yang Ming-Yi. 1991. *The Journey of Meng.* New York: Dial Books.

Scieszka, Jon. Illustrated by Lane Smith. 1989. *The True Story of the 3 Little Pigs.* New York: Viking Kestrel.

Seeger, Pete. Illustrated by Michael Hays. 1986. *Abiyoyo.* New York: Macmillan.

Sheldon, Dyan. Illustrated by Gary Blythe. 1990. *The Whale's Song.* New York: Dial Books.

Steig, William. 1990. *Shrek.* New York: Farrar, Straus, Giroux.

Turnbull, Ann. Illustrated by Michael Foreman. 1989. *The Sand Horse.* New York: Macmillan.

Yolen, Jane. Illustrated by Charles Mikolaycak. 1990. *Tam Lin.* New York: HBJ.

Further References

Henderson, Kathy. 1990. *Market Guide for Young Artists and Photographers.* Crozet, VA: Shoe Tree Press.

Henderson, Kathy. 1990. *Market Guide for Young Writers.* Crozet, VA: Shoe Tree Press.

Hickman, Janet and Cullinan, Bernice, ed. 1989. *Children's Literature in the Classroom: Weaving Charlotte's Web.* Boston: Christopher-Gordon Publishers.

Huck, Charlotte S., ed. 1979. *Children's Literature in the Elementary School.* New York: Holt, Rinehart and Winston.

Moir, Hughes, Cain, Melissa and Prosak-Beres, Leslie, ed. 1990. *Collected Perspectives: Choosing and Using Books for the Classroom.* Boston: Christopher-Gordon Publishers.

O'Sullivan, Colleen. 1988. *The Challenge of Picture Books.* Melbourne: Thomas Nelson Australia.

Trelease, Jim. 1984. *The Read-Aloud Handbook.* New York: Penguin.

Other Resources

The New Advocate
Christopher-Gordon Publishers
P. O. Box 809
Needham Heights, MA 02194-0006

(A *magazine "for those involved with young people and their literature." Frequently publishes articles about, or by, children's authors and illustrators.*)

Landmark Editions, Inc.
P. O. Box 4469
1402 Kansas Ave.
Kansas City, Missouri 64127

(*Runs "The National Written and Illustrated By . . . Awards Contest for Students"*)

8

Picture Books After Eighth Grade

David Ludlam

Over the past twenty-five years as a high school English teacher I have come to the realization that school reading material does not have to be limited to the classics and that there is much to be gained from the use of contemporary literature. However, I really never considered children's picture books as secondary-school reading matter until a discussion in our teachers' workroom started me thinking of how they could be used in the English curriculum.

Our guidance department had recently established a support group for pregnant and parenting teens. One afternoon a group of teachers was meeting to assist in the selection of books for our school library, and the conversation turned to how we could help the support group. We were gathered around a catalogue-strewn table. A poster on the wall portrayed a young child holding a book in an outstretched hand with the caption "Read me a story."

"I wonder if our students recognize the importance of reading to their children?" I asked the others.

"With the expense of everything today," Judy, another member of the English department responded, "I'm not sure that they could afford the books."

"What about the public library?" Bert suggested. "They have a great children's room."

"Your town might have a great children's room," Ann, our librarian, replied, "but my town has a one-room library with a moth-eaten set of the *Britanica* and some old *National Geographics*; plus, it's only open on Wednesday mornings! A lot of our students come from towns where the libraries have closed completely."

"What about us?" I asked. "Why don't we set up a section of children's books in our school library so that students can borrow them to take home and read to their kids?"

Anne said that she did not object to spending some of her budget on children's books, and Karen added that the guidance department could also come up with some funds. As the idea took hold, we browsed through the book catalogues and drew up a list of children's books.

"Oh, I just loved *Curious George*, and so did my son," Judy said waxing nostalgic over a picture in one of the catalogues. "I think Bobby was even better at getting into trouble than that monkey was!"

"My kid liked *In the Night Kitchen*." Bert, a History teacher added showing the picture in the catalogue to the group. "I think these guys look just like Oliver Hardy."

"They're meant to," Judy explained. "Sendak said that he based them on Laurel and Hardy, but that Stan was too thin for the image he wanted."

"I think Tomie dePaola's illustrations are wonderful," Ann said. "Did you know that he illustrated a book on the folklore of marriage?"

"Where's the *Little Engine That Could*?" asked the Science teacher, "I used to love that one when I was a kid."

The children's picture book section of the library would complement a selection of what Ann called "mature readers' picture books," which was already in use by the English department. I had developed a half-year writing unit based on life in eighteenth-century New England. It included field trips to Old Sturbridge Village, Salem, and Old Deerfield. The writing project required the students to create a family and record the events of their lives in a journal. The students became immersed in background material about the time period. After reviewing countless reference and history books on the period, I realized that most of them contained lengthy descriptions but almost no illustrations. To help alleviate the problem, our school librarian and I visited the bookstores at the various historical sites in our area and started buying children's picture books to expand the library's reference collection with sources that contained good illustrations of the colonial era.

At first my students ignored these books, which they labeled "for little kids," but as desperation to include description in their family journals grew, they quietly and covertly turned to the picture books. In the end, as their journals became filled with wonderful images of colonial life, they openly and actively shared the books and discussed the illustrations. From then on, picture books became a mainstay of my historical writing units. We went on to the Civil War and the Industrial Revolution, gaining images for stories from various children's picture books.

The success of those books in my historical writing units led me to consider how to include them in some of my other classes. Many of my students were what is called academically nonmotivated or reluctant learners, especially where English literature was concerned. I had been searching for material that these students could read and discuss but which would also pertain to their lives. Abridged or condensed books had been an utter failure, and most of the low-level/high-interest books were actually very boring and demeaning to them. I turned to children's picture books as a possible solution to the dilemma. I was aware that the students might consider reading children's books an insult both to their age and intelligence; however, I felt that these books, especially the picture books, are a very real part of our culture. Many of my students had not been read to nor experienced storytelling at home. Much of their knowledge of stories came from television and VCRs. I hoped that my course could begin to help my students fill in the gaps and develop a new excitement about reading.

My approach was to explain to the students that it was a course for parents, which a few of them already were, and many of them one day would become. The course offered a real purpose for the students to become acquainted with children's books. Secondly, the material was suitable for my students to evaluate various literary aspects. It turned out to be the right approach; as one of the students later explained to members of his class, "I've never read any of this stuff before. At first I thought it was baby stuff, but when Mr. Ludlam said that one day we might have kids of our own, it made sense to me that I should know about these books."

Near the end of the unit, the students were asked to discuss what they felt they had gained from the course. Three of the students who in the beginning had strongly resisted the unit were sitting together at one of the tables in my classroom. Here is what they had to say:

Hector, a non-native speaker with limited English reading ability said, "I read this book *Where the Wild Things Are* to my mother and brother, and she laughed. She said that Max was just like me when I was little. I started to teach my little brother how to read the book. He's five and is going to preschool. My mother doesn't read English so she can't help him much. He liked the pictures and followed along with me while I read the words."

"My favorite was *Dear Mili*," Karen explained. "My mom died four years ago and . . . well, the book helped. It really got us talking in class and, and that helped me think about it."

Bob, one of our more vocal school resisters, said, "I've got a list of books I'm gonna read to my kid when I have one. They're all the books I've read and liked. We've talked about how important it is to read to young kids. A lot of us were never read to when we were young. It's gonna be different with my own kid."

At another table Carol, Mike, Aaron, and Melody were discussing various books they had read. Each had become an expert on one particular author.

"My mother told me that *Madeline* was one of her favorite books when she was young," Carol told the others.

"So? I still think it's a kids' book!" Mike returned. "It's something like my little sister would read."

"Bemelmans isn't just a kids' author," Carol retorted. "He wrote a lot of books for adults too."

"I don't think that Sendak is just a kids' author either," Aaron interjected. "He puts a lot of stuff in his books that's meant for adults. In that book on famous illustrators he said that fantasy isn't just limited to kids."

"I think that all really good children's books are also meant for adults," Melody offered.

"Right," Mike said sarcastically, "*Babar the Elephant* and *Curious George* are for adults!"

"In a way, yes, They have to be," Melody persisted. "How could a mother read a book over and over again to her child if she didn't also like it? I think the author has to write a children's book on two levels, so that both kids and adults will enjoy it. Who do you think buys the books, anyway!"

This children's literature class became a place of reading, sharing, and conversation. When a student selected a book for study, she or he would share it with the others in the class. It would be read aloud and discussed. Students acted as reviewers and wrote brief summaries and evaluations of the books on index cards, which went into their files. For many of the less able readers in the class the picture books represented the first success they had experienced with reading and discussing literature. Prior to this unit many of my students did not finish books they started. Their class participation was often limited and wrought with embarrassment. With the picture book course, some things changed; my students were able to read, finish, and understand what they read. Class participation became so lively that I found it necessary to use small discussion groups to give all students the opportunity to express their views.

My student teacher, Lori Barnett, conferred with me about the difficulty she was experiencing in her ninth-grade writing class. She said she was struggling with helping her students develop their writing. As she put it, "My students are excellent at telling stories, but when it comes to writing them down, they don't know the first thing about structure. I suppose that students who don't read books just don't have the literary experience to draw upon for examples." She had observed what I had been doing with the picture book unit and decided to see if picture books might help her students with their writing. She wanted her students to understand the structure of stories so that they could write a short story of their own. She introduced the picture books not necessarily as literature appropriate to the students' reading and interest levels but as short, easy examples of stories that the students could quickly read and then discuss in one class period.

"I needed a way to get from the present back into time for my ghost town story," Tony explained. "It's what Ms. Barnett calls a transition. In the *Polar Express* the transition is the train. It takes the boy from his house to the North Pole. I really liked the story and the way it ended with the sleigh bell in the box that only the children could hear. I'm going to have my story end by having a wanted poster appear in the deserted jail, but it will be just like new rather than old."

"I wanted to write a folktale," Carla explained, "but we don't have much storytelling in my family. I don't have any grandparents and my mom doesn't remember much about her gram, other than she worked a lot. So Ms. Barnett had me read *Mirandy and Brother Wind* [Patricia McKissack]. It was wonderful! The girl is just like my little sister."

"I like poetry and wanted to do a long poem like *The Giving Tree* [Shel Silverstein]," Stacy related, "but it was too long, so I used some ideas from *Where the Sidewalk Ends* [Shel Silverstein]. Silverstein uses great pictures to go with his poems. It's OK to have pictures with stories, so I'm going to draw pictures to go with my poems. He [Silverstein] did it and it's not babyish at all."

"Have you ever read *Song and Dance Man* [Karen Ackerman]?" Terry asked. "It's this great story about some kids and their old grandfather who had been a song and dance man in the theatre. It gave me a great idea for a story about my own grandfather. He's always talking about what he did in the war. I went home and talked to him about World War II, and I'm writing this story about an old guy who has this trunk full of stuff from the war out in his garage. As he tells his story to the kids and takes stuff out of the old trunk, the story will go back to World War II in France."

"Dialogue is very difficult for many students to understand," Ms. Barnett explained, "but with picture books I can show a variety of examples. We've even borrowed some of the big books because they work better than using an overhead transparency."

Another use for picture books in the secondary school can be found in our tenth-grade English classes where a research paper is required of all students. For the ESL students and the less able readers this project has always been a point of anxiety and frustration for students and teachers alike. The research papers are supervised by the English department but done in coordination with either the science or social studies teachers. After years of reading verbatim transcripts from encyclopedias, the teachers sat down with the school librarian to discuss the situation. The initial result was an introductory unit taught by the librarian on the use of the library in the finding of information. But it still did not solve the problem completely. For many students encyclopedias remained their sole source of information.

In the end, the teachers decided that the library's collection of books containing research information was too threatening or difficult for many students to read and comprehend. The solution came accidentally when one ESL student chose the subject of castles for his paper and brought into school some books from his town library. Among them were David Macaulay's *Castle*, Aliki's *A Medieval Feast*, and Goodall's *The Story of a Castle* (a wordless book). Someone in his town library had helped the student find books that he could read and that were filled with information that would be useful for his project. A conversation about it in the teachers' lounge sent the science teacher off to the elementary and junior high school collections and his own town library. He enthusiastically returned with cartons of wonderfully illustrated books filled with very accurate information.

Over the next year our school librarian began ordering social studies and science related children's picture books and illustrated books, both fictional and informational. They ranged from *The Way Things Work* by David Macaulay and *Fossils Tell of Long Ago* by Aliki to *Colonial Living* by Edward Tunis. The books were not singled out but were shelved right along with the rest of the collection. As part of the term paper unit, all tenth graders were given instruction on the use of the library and then were free to select the books of their choice. The picture books appeared on the working bibliographies of a majority of the students, both proficient and less proficient readers, thus there was little stigma about their use.

"The wonderful thing about it," said the Science teacher, "is that the kids now write papers in their own words. I don't have to grade encyclopedias any longer! I used to get so sick of feeling I had to give a passing grade to a student I felt had copied an encyclopedia because he used the proper format for his paper."

It should be noted that not all students produced great examples of high school level research papers, but what they wrote now was their own work. It represented thought and understanding, even if it was only five pages discussing the life cycle of a moth. We found for the most part the content, all compiled from children's picture books, was accurate, and the students had learned something about both the subject matter and the process of preparing a library research paper.

Establishing a library collection of picture books for teenage parents, using picture books in a literature class, looking to picture books as a source for models in writing class, and offering informational picture books to students attempting research papers provide four examples of the many possible ways picture books can be used successfully with older students. Yet it must remain clear that at no time are the picture books being used solely because they provide easy reading material. Admittedly, for many of our students these picture books do represent print written at a level that is easily accessible; however, we feel it inappropriate to use picture books as texts in a basic or remedial reading class. This would both undermine the students' sense of themselves as young adults and diminish the inherent value of the books.

In the case of the eleventh-grade English class, picture books were studied as a genre. They were analyzed for their use in reading to young children. Many educators recognize the importance of reading to young children and of early, preschool literacy experience (Smith, 1985; Harste, Woodward, & Burke, 1984; and Goodman, 1986). For many of our high school students, this experience was nonexistent. Introducing them to children's picture books, and how to use them, may well save the next generation from the negative and frustrating school experiences of their parents.

The high school lending library of children's picture books not only gives parenting teens material to read with their children, but also offers other students the opportunity to read and share the books with younger siblings or even older family members.

The informational picture books and historical picture books shelved with the regular collection in the library offer a range of materials for readers of all abilities. In some cases the teachers or librarian may direct a student with limited reading ability to a certain topic choice or subject area where picture book material is available. Often the quality of children's picture books is far superior to the edited and simplified language versions of adult books. One benefit derived from including these books in the library collection is that all students can participate equally in the library research process.

In the writing classroom, understanding the structure and style of stories becomes possible when students can browse through picture books. They offer students the opportunity to look at a wide variety of styles and genres over a short period of time. In a single class period a teacher can read and discuss a complete story or two with students, pointing out various methods and means of telling a story. Big books (very large format picture books) supply the teacher with a colorful, large teaching aid through which she or he can demonstrate the form and use of dialogue, paragraphing, and punctuation, as well as share a good story. Picture books also offer samples of genre and style such as folk tales, fantasy, historical fiction, first-person monologues, poetry, and third-person narration.

Atwell (1987), Calkins (1986), Graves (1983), and others point out the need for children to write and share their writing with their peers. Books give the students ideas and concepts for their writing. In addition, talking about and analyzing picture books in class under a teacher's guidance provides a model of the process to be used when talking about one another's writing as students work on and share their stories in peer writing groups.

Providing all students with equal access to sources of information is important in our schools. Too often students are offered texts that are inaccessible to them, thus limiting their comprehension and excluding them from discussion. Children's picture books can help to eliminate the educational barrier that prevents less able students from finding appropriate texts from which to learn.

Throughout this discussion of picture books I have purposefully avoided the topic of illustration. I did not want to dwell on what of course is one of the most clear advantages of these books—that of the connection between word and picture. As the old adage goes, "One picture is worth a thousand words." This can be especially true for students with reading difficulties, where the picture may well offer an aid to gaining meaning from the text. Though my purpose here was not to discuss remedial reading, I cannot help but remember a particular incident where picture books made an important difference for a student.

Phil was an eleventh-grade, special education student who at age nineteen could not read simple directions or write down a telephone message that he could later decipher. I would often see him sitting in the school library while he was waiting for his special-needs tutor. He would be intently looking at magazines that I knew he could not read. One day as I was browsing through the periodical section I asked him what he was reading.

"I'm looking at this magazine about Maine," he said holding up a copy of *Down East*. "My mom and I go there each summer to visit my grandparents."

We talked about Maine for a few minutes, and I told him that we had a collection of books in the library about New England and the seacoast. I took him over to the librarian and asked her to suggest some books for him. Phil had hidden his illiteracy well and would never have embarrassed himself by refusing to look at the books she offered. She took him to a bookcase filled with travel books, sea stories, and New England lore. There were thick volumes of print, glossy photograph books, and various illustrated books including some children's picture books that had been on loan from our city library.

A few days later I saw Phil again in the library, though this time he was seated off in a corner intensely bent over a book. I sat down beside him and noted that he was reading Barbara Cooney's *Island Boy*.

"Good book?" I asked.

He started to shove it aside but realized that hiding it was foolish seeing that we were both looking at its open pages. "Yah, it reminds me of my grandpa. He lives on Deer Isle in Maine. It's a good story even if it is for kids. I'd like to sail on a boat like the Six Brothers sometime.

"My grandfather was from Maine," I said. "He gave up lobstering and came down here to be a carpenter. Matthais reminds me a lot of him. He used to tell me stories about his life in Maine. I've got a copy of this book at home."

"For your kids?" he asked.

"No, for me." I replied.

Works Cited

Atwell, Nancie. 1987. *In the Middle: Writing, Reading, and Learning with Adolescents*. Portsmouth, NH: Heinemann.

Calkins, Lucy McCormick. 1986. *The Art of Teaching Writing*. Portsmouth, NH: Heinemann.

Goodman, Kenneth. 1986. *What's Whole About Whole Language*. Portsmouth, NH: Heinemann.

Graves, Donald H. 1983. *Writing: Teachers and Children at Work*. Portsmouth, NH: Heinemann.

Harste, Jerome; Virginia Woodward; and Carolyn Burke. 1984. *Language Stories and Literacy Lessons*. Portsmouth, NH: Heinemann.

Smith, Frank. 1985. *Reading Without Nonsense*. New York: Teachers College.

9

Invitations from the Librarian: Picture Books for Older Children

Carolyn K. Jenks

A school library offers an excellent opportunity to expose children to the many-splendored world of picture books. Since our school houses students from kindergarten through grade five, and since I have been there for a long time, I have imparted my high regard for picture books to many students from the beginning to the end of their elementary school careers. Many intermediate students value picture books and have no inhibition about going to the shelves where many of them are kept.

The placement of picture books in the library affects not only accessibility, but their use pattern as well. The picture story book section comprises the largest group of picture books, the rest being found throughout the remaining library collection, according to subject or kind. Librarians do not always agree about where to locate many picture books. If the story is in rhyme, should it be in the picture story section or the poetry section? If it is a counting book, should it be in the math section? If it is about wildflowers and has very little text, should it be in the science section? The librarian must put a book where it will be most easily found by most of the library patrons. Whatever decision is made, it is important that they be able to find a book easily, free of arrangement that might offend their dignity. Certainly, any grouping of books by grade level would run the risk of deterring intermediate students from reading picture books. The arrangement of library materials makes a statement. I want ours to say, "Welcome, come in! All of the materials are here for you to explore. Browse and search; if you have difficulty, we will help you."

The reasons picture books might be used by intermediate students are many, but the reason of sheer enjoyment is probably the most compelling of all. Often they revisit a book like an old friend that they may have read or heard "a long, *long* time ago when I was in kindergarten." In addition to enjoying it again, they can measure their progress. Many students have told me with amazement that this *easy* book was one they couldn't even read when they were in first grade. Sometimes their pleasure is enhanced by additional experience or knowledge gained over the years. *Madeline*'s (Ludwig Bemelmans) exotic life in an orphanage and her scary and famous experience with appendicitis are usually appreciated by young children. Older children are also intrigued with these things, but in addition may be aware that Madeline's Paris is the real thing and can pick out the Eiffel Tower and other more obscure landmarks in Bemelmans' dashing, Gallic illustrations. Sometimes it is an author who captures a student's interest: I once saw two fifth-grade boys pull out all the books by Bill Peet and talk excitedly about their favorites. When they were in first grade, they could borrow one book at a time, but now that they were in fifth, they could take out five: this meant, that day, five Peets for each of them!

A picture story book can embody the essential literary elements of any story. Since our goals in the library include instilling the appreciation of literary structure, we examine as many aspects of a book as we can to discover what makes a story the way it is. Looking at a picture book that provides good examples of plot, characterization, style, setting, theme, and point of view is an excellent, accessible way to begin the study of elements of literature.

For young students, plot is probably the most understandable literary element. In much of their writing, and in their choices of books, "what happens" is everything. I've offered beautifully written stories to students, only to hear them say, "But nothing *happens*!" You have to begin with the action. One of my favorite plot lessons occurred while reading *Rosie's Walk* (Pat Hutchins) to a group of such students. I read it without showing the pictures. "What happens" is that a hen journeys around the barnyard and goes home again. The end. "Isn't that a great story?" I say. My listeners tell me it was short and boring and not really a story at all. Then I read it while sharing the pictures. Now they see that there's a hungry, bumbling fox who's after this innocent hen. That Rosie makes it home at all becomes an amazing accomplishment heightened by the fact that she will never know, as we do, how many close calls she had. Hutchins has chosen to add character, excitement, and humor through illustration.

Point of view is a literary element that, when brought to students' attention, nearly always piques their interest. Who has not been offended at hearing a slanted account of an incident by a partner in crime who wanted to look less bad? *I'll Fix Anthony* (Judith Viorst) is told from the point of view of a younger brother who feels disenfranchised and who is so hopeful and naive that he doesn't realize that Anthony will always be older and that his elaborate plans of revenge may be fruitless. The reader sees Anthony from the younger brother's point of view. How would Anthony himself describe the same situation? Sometimes we have the pleasure and insight of hearing the same story from more than one point of view. Almost everyone has heard *The Three Little Pigs*. Some students are interested to discover that Walt Disney could not countenance the idea of anyone being eaten or boiled, so in his version the pigs and wolf run away rather than confront each other. The implications of these differences are good for a lively discussion. Now, add the point of view of the wolf, who, thanks to Jon Scieszka in *The True Story of the Little Pigs*! finally has equal time. Satire, irony, and humor can be talked about here as well.

Wonderful examples of character development abound in picture books. Even though there is not a word contained in *The Grey Lady and the Strawberry Snatcher* (Molly Bang), the creative confidence of the grey lady unfolds as she deftly eludes her crafty pursuer. Characters who develop and change in short picture books are difficult to create successfully, but it can be done. *A Special Trade* (Sally Wittman), effects change by the passage of time. Old Bartholomew spends time caring for his young neighbor, Nelly, when she is very small. When he is old, there comes a time when Nelly needs to take care of him. The girl has grown into a caring person who is happy to be able to help someone who helped her.

Style is yet another topic. How many words does an author need to get a story across to the reader? Not many, if it's *Fish for Supper* by M. B. Goffstein. A simple, straightforward story about fishing in the daily life of one grandmother is reinforced by equally simple line drawings. Not a word or line is unnecessary in the text and illustrations. On the other hand, Carl Sandburg requires a lot of words to describe *The Wedding Procession of the Rag Doll and the Broom Handle and Who Was in It* (illustrated by Harriet Pincus). Even the title is excessive, and the great nonsensical description goes on from there.

Dealing with setting is sometimes problematic to intermediate readers. *Millions of Cats* (Wanda Gag) effectively describes the little house of the very old woman and the very old man in a few words: no more are needed. But *The River Bank* (the first chapter of *The Wind in the Willows* by Kenneth Grahame and illustrated by Adrienne Adams) is such a many-faceted place that the author needs to say a great deal about it to make sure the reader gets the full effect. Students will never agree on how much description of setting is necessary, but examining setting and its importance in various picture books is a way to look at the effect it has on the story as a whole.

It is easy for the theme of a book to be moralistic or obvious. Sometimes that's a good way to begin talking about it. Jean de La

Fontaine's *The Lion and the Rat*, illustrated by Brian Wildsmith, comes right out and gives the moral at the end of the story. William Steig's *Amos and Boris* bears the similar theme of being able to help even if one is small, but here it is enlarged to include the virtues of friendship, kindness, and devotion. Indeed, this story of the mouse and the whale who have an adventure on the high seas provides a successful rendering of all of the literary elements I have just discussed.

Some of these elements, certainly style, theme, and point of view, are also important in the examination of informational picture books, but probably at the top of the list are accuracy and clarity, both in text and in illustration.

A fourth-grade boy once brought me what I considered to be a pretty good bird identification book and said, "Does that look like a scissor-tailed flycatcher to you?" Not good enough, apparently! In this case, we needed to look at several bird books to compare them and accepted what the majority of sources purported to be the truth. In discussing accuracy and clarity of illustration, it is interesting to think about drawings versus photographs. In recent years more and more books have been illustrated with color photographs. It seems logical that they would be more accurate, and I know many students who don't believe a picture is real unless it's a photograph. The clarity of a photograph and its appropriateness to the subject are important. *Rocks and Minerals* (R. F. Symes), one of the Eyewitness Books, is full of clear, color photographs and short descriptions of all kinds of rocks for collectors and researchers. One can read all the small print, or just look at the beautiful array of colors and textures. There are some fine examples of accuracy in drawings as well. The meticulous line drawings of David Macaulay in *Castle* take the reader into, over, under, and around a medieval castle, which is a composite of various Welsh castles built between 1277 and 1305. *Bugs* (Joan Wright) is illustrated with the precise, color drawings of Nancy Winslow Parker. Her careful research has resulted in such impressive examples as a five-inch flea, drawn exactly to scale. All parts are labelled, and next to the creature is a small line showing the actual size of an average flea.

Accuracy and clarity of text in picture books is more prevalent than some students believe. For instance, a student doing a report on an animal might outline the following requirements for a book: It must be (1) a whole book about that animal only; (2) pretty short; (3) accurate, clear, colored photographs; (4) an index; and (5) a subdivided text that matches exactly the questions of the report writer: habitat, food, enemies, body parts, gestation period, life span. Wait. This sounds a lot like an encyclopedia article that students are discouraged from using. There are books that more or less fit this description, and students will find them. My job as a librarian is to persuade them that there are *other* books as well that contain such facts but that also convey a spirit of excitement and inquiry that may inspire the reader to do further research. *Wild Mouse* (Irene Brady) is the illustrated journal of the author-artist's encounter with a mouse seen darting across her sink top. During two months of observation, the mouse is discovered to be a female who gives birth to a litter. The book doesn't give all the facts about the life of the mouse, but it does give the facts of reproduction with beautiful, accurate drawings, as well as a sense of the author's wonder and discovery. Joanna Cole has written a series of books about the bodies of various animals, of which *A Horse's Body* is one. She examines the construction of the body and how it enables the animal to do the things it does. It is compared with the human body to make the information more understandable and illustrated with black and white photographs and clear line drawings. Each of these animal books needs to be used with others to get the complete picture, but they give information from such interesting viewpoints that the reader may care to look for more good books about the subject. *People* (Peter Spier) is a book that has led many of our students to all kinds of things. From the double-page spread of Adam and Eve in the garden of Eden, the scene is changed to the billions of people in the world today. This book makes students wonder about population explosion, races, countries, life styles, food, religions, poverty, languages, etc. From this book they can go in any number of directions toward a deeper understanding of the uniqueness of human beings.

Teaching reference and research skills to intermediate students is facilitated by the existence of good picture books. In addition to the possibilities already mentioned, picture books can be used to widen the traditional "look-it-up-and-get-the-facts" techniques. Our fifth graders have sometimes embarked on large research projects in which they pretend to travel in groups across the United States by various routes. Their job is to find out about places on their journey. Everybody knows about the encyclopedias, the books on individual states, and the geographical dictionary. But what about moving on from there and putting some pizzazz into the report that will make classmates happy to read it? In travelling to New York City one might use Betsy Maestro's large, colorful *The Story of the Statue of Liberty*, which not only tells us that the statue was transferred in 214 crates from Paris to New York, but also shows the contents of one of them (maybe it's a piece of her dress; maybe it's her nose). *Paddle-to-the-Sea* (Holling C. Holling) is a wooden figure in a canoe, whose water journey takes him through the Great Lakes. This is a story that includes much information in the text and the illustrations. In the margins are bits of information, such as a labelled diagram of the workings of a canal lock. A biography of *Buffalo Bill* by Ingri and Edgar d'Aulaire takes us from Iowa where he was born, to somewhere near Denver, Colorado where he died. And in the humorous single edition of *Casey At the Bat*, illustrated by Wallace Tripp, we find that San Francisco, of all places, was where Ernest Thayer wrote his quintessential poem of baseball in 1888. The possibilities are limited only by the imagination and creativity of the searcher. I try to give them some ideas, hoping that they'll continue by themselves.

There are so many good picture books, fiction and nonfiction, that with a little imagination one can weave them into a study of nearly any subject. In fact, we need them to enrich the fabric of our findings, to add color, to provide for the reluctant reader, and to bring the group together.

Our fifth graders were studying Native Americans with a vengeance (is that a fifth-grade, mid-year learning style?). They came through the library like locusts, signing out all the information books they could find. Then they came through and got all the Native American fiction. My job, in addition to locating material, was to listen to their excited discoveries and to try to contribute what I could. The theme that kept unfolding was the importance of tradition and strength of spirit. We looked at these themes in biographies of Native Americans, in various kinds of fiction including Olaf Baker's haunting *Where the Buffaloes Begin*. This story of a boy who needs to find what he's heard over and over again in a legend, goes on a long ride to a place where the buffalo are rising out of a misty lake. Is it real? Was he dreaming? Does it matter? As the students found out more and more about these people, they could begin to accept writings that concerned the spirit. As the study was ending, I talked about Native American legends and folktales. Preparing for this, I found a Tuscarora tale that reminded me of so many things we'd talked about that I knew I had to read it aloud to the class: *When the Corn is Red* by Pekay Shor. This one short tale portrays a way of life, a rocky relationship with the Great Spirit, and the deep sadness concerning the coming of the white people, which will change the lives of the Native Americans—not forever, says the Great Spirit, but until the corn is red again. It was ironic to read this story just before Thanksgiving, but as full of truths and implications as it was, it provided a valuable exercise.

Since we live near the ocean, our students study the salt water environment in nearly every grade. Fortunately, there are books on this subject at all levels. For the older student who has difficulty with reading and for the student whose native language is not English, the wealth of picture books provides a way to participate. *Down to the Beach* written by May Garelick and illustrated by Barbara Cooney gives a poetic introduction to the beach with its creatures and happenings; the text and watercolors provide atmosphere and information. *Along the Seashore* (Margaret Buck) is more precise. It is more difficult to read, but if a student has found a sea urchin shell and wants to know about it, he can use this book as a reference guide. The black and white drawings are clear and detailed, so that the sea urchin shell looks precisely like the ones found at the shore. Black and white photographs take the reader aboard a lobster boat in Maine in *Finestkind O'Day* by Bruce McMillan. The process of lobstering is seen up close, complete with gulls, waves, and the good nature of a lobsterman who is taking a young boy out for the day. *The Salt Marsh* by Virginia Schonborg is a small book of poems illustrated with line drawings of the marsh and its creatures. It provides a different way of looking, making the reader aware of the still tallness of the great blue heron and the quickness of the scuttling, small crab.

The attempt to enrich the experiences of intermediate students with picture books would be more difficult if I had to do it all by myself. I am fortunate to work with teachers who value books and who are broad-minded and creative enough to include picture books in all parts of their programs. The general shift away from textbooks and toward trade books makes the library more central and the cooperation between teacher and librarian more obviously necessary. Teachers accompany their classes to the library, and we all work together to accomplish our educational purposes. These teachers are as likely as I am to come rushing in with a great new picture book to edify or amuse.

Picture books are for everyone. I enjoy sharing them with adults and noticing what they read. Someone who finally got his Ph.D. in management science received a copy of *If I Ran the Circus* by Dr. Seuss. A sports loving man read the outrageously humorous *How Tom Beat Captain Najork and His Hired Sportsmen* by Russell Hoban, illustrated by Quentin Blake, to his wife and grown children during cocktail hour. An eighty-two-year-old woman who swims every day thoroughly enjoyed Kathyrn Lasky's *Sea Swan*, especially the illustration of the seventy-five-year-old grandmother in her new emerald green swimsuit. Indeed, picture books are important to me. There's a huge pine tree in my neighborhood that reminds me of one of Marc Simont's paintings in *A Tree Is Nice* (Janice Udry). Or is it the picture that reminds me of the tree? I like them both for what they give to each other in my mind.

The world of picture books goes on and on. The richness to be found in them can be used and appreciated by anyone who discovers them. The growing variety of picture books makes it more and more possible for librarians to invite children of all ages to partake and enjoy.

10

Using Picture Books To Promote the Learning of Science

Phyllis E. Brazee

I am a victim of rote memorization science instruction. I am a global learner who needs to see the larger picture and then relate details to that picture. For twenty-five years I have felt that I could not be a scientist, that I couldn't even think as a scientist. I have spent much of my time reading and writing narrative material. As a teacher, I have come to realize that many of us in elementary education, both professors and undergraduate education students, feel this way about science (and math and social science and technology). I didn't used to go looking for science in my world: now, I do. Why? I have team taught with science education professors for four years and have discovered what science *really* is: it is wonder about the world, curiosity, and endless questions.

Is science restricted to only a chosen few? No. It is a gift to humanity. It is innate in every human being. How do I know? I remember my two sons and all their friends at age two, three, four—before they went to school. They were nonstop wonder machines—Why, Mommy? Why, Daddy? Why, why, why? What were their questions like? They were just like those found in the delightful book, *Why?* by Kathie Billingslea Smith: "Why do things that go up always come down?" Does this kind of question sound familiar to you?

What happened to that native curiosity we all were born with? School happened. School where there was always only one right answer, where only the fast responders were rewarded, where "nonsense," as Frank Smith (1985) describes it so well, was taught, drilled, memorized, and forgotten.

Did I do well in chemistry? Yes, I passed the New York State Regents Exam with a decent score, but can I predict today how household cooking substances will work? Can I really explain the function of baking soda or powder to my young son, the baker, who has forgotten to put it into his first batch of homemade pretzels and is devastated? No.

Did my physics training prepare me to take over at the helm of our little sailboat if anything should happen, navigate us home through shifting winds and changing waves? Where is the knowledge from the wave machine I know we studied in high school physics? Would that knowledge even apply to this situation? Where did I learn about angles, about velocity, and wind direction?

How humbled I am about what I don't remember, and what I probably was never even exposed to about earth science as I travel across our incredible country. The first time we went West, in our VW-van version of the covered wagon, I can remember being completely shocked, coming from the never-ending plains of Nebraska and eastern Colorado, at the vision of the Rocky Mountains ahead of us, marching from left to right out of sight on each end. How did they get there? How did people ever survive the shock of them to find a way through them?

As I raise my two sons, I am often painfully aware of how much I have forgotten of the information I memorized over my sixteen years of public school and college life science classes. When a child is sick at two in the morning, what do I do? What is normal treatment? Why do I feel so helpless? Why shouldn't I know what to do, or at least try?

Am I a science illiterate today? No. Why? Many events and people over the last four years have rekindled in me the native curiosity I had as a child. In working with science educators for four years, I have discovered for the first time that science is everywhere around me. Every waking moment of my life, I am learning about the science in my world. I am asking questions just like three- and four-year-olds.

Undergraduate Elementary Education Majors

Each semester my teammate and I have solicited responses from our students before we begin our integrated language arts/science course. It is important for us to know about the attitudes they hold. Overwhelmingly, they say

> To be honest, teaching science scares me.
>
> I believe science is important, however, I don't know if I know enough to be able to teach it adequately. My science self-concept is low.

> Teaching reading and writing doesn't scare me as much as the thought of teaching science. My science background, at best, is weak. I don't know how to make science interesting and fun for kids because it was never presented to me in that way.

Many feel as the third student does: confident in themselves as a reader and writer, and confident as a teacher of reading and writing. Most, like me, however, feel very inadequate as scientists and science teachers.

I want my undergraduates to learn that they can think as scientists do because, as scientists do, they observe their world; they engage in everyday science experiments after making hypotheses, all in the course of their daily lives. I want my students to recognize the scientific questions they ask each day, as all four-year-olds do. I want my students to recapture their own wonder about the world. Without that, they will continue to be afraid of science, and most likely avoid teaching it. They also will not recognize and support the scientist in each of their students. This cannot continue as we move into the information age of the twenty-first century.

Using Picture Books as a Way to Rekindle Scientific Curiosity

Early in my team teaching career, I modeled the read-aloud process for my students using Peter Parnall's book, *Winter Barn*. My teammate, Warren Tomkiewicz, sat in the back of our classroom, a pen moving rapidly across a piece of paper. After the students and I had discussed the book and the read-aloud process, Warren asked: "What science concepts did anyone recognize in that book?" The room was silent. No one, including me, had given science a thought as we sat enthralled by Parnall's book. Warren then read a list he had made during my reading. He had identified thirty-five separate science concepts in that book. Warren helped my students and me see literature—narrative—from a different point of view: specifically, as curious, wondering scientists.

Due to the shared insights of Warren and other science educators I have since worked with, my students and I now spend quite a bit of time revisiting favorite narrative picture books with an eye to the potential science concepts they hold. Any one of these concepts can then be the springboard into a science lesson, experiment, or unit of study.

One such book is Robert McCloskey's *Time of Wonder*. This book portrays a special summer on the coast of Maine. Many of us read this book over and over again to our students over the years without ever focusing on the extensive science involved in the book. Now, however, I am struck by the realization that scientific knowledge actually serves as the setting of the book, is part of the plot, and provides the theme of the story. After reading this book, my students and I could pause and investigate:

- Geography related to coastal islands, or Maine's place in the country
- Weather including clouds, rain, fog, and hurricanes; sea life including such animals as porpoises, seals, crabs, etc.
- Wave motion.
- The life cycle.
- Astronomy.
- The seasons.
- Habits of birds.

Any one or several of these could be explored in a science methods class, providing students with references for related activities and experiments. McCloskey's book closes with a classic child-scientist question: "Where do hummingbirds go in a hurricane?"

When Elementary Teachers Feel Inadequate in Their Science Knowledge

My students and I talk extensively about how specific science concepts could be investigated more thoroughly in children's picture books. Our problem, however, is almost always rooted in our poor self-confidence as scientists and our lack of knowledge of science concepts. As I have worked over the years with my science education teammates, I have come to realize how many science misconceptions my students and I have acquired. What can we do about this? Here are some solutions we have developed to date.

Elementary teachers who feel inadequate in science should not be afraid to admit it. Further, they should feel comfortable seeking information from peers, either in their building or at the middle school or high school level, who love science. The easiest way to do this would be to share several read-aloud selections with these teachers (experts), ask them to read or listen to the stories with a science ear, and then to share what the science concepts are, where teachers can get further information, and what actual hands-on science experiences would be appropriate for their elementary students.

Although there are many science experiment and activity books now available for elementary teachers to use to extend their science exploration in picture books, relatively few of them actually explain the science concepts underlying the experiments and activities. Instead they seem to be recipes with no actual discussion of the science involved. Therefore, teachers should be aware of those experiment and activity books that do explain underlying science concepts. Teachers should seek these out and make sure they are available in classroom or school libraries. Several excellent titles include: Alison Alexander and Susie Bower, *Science Magic: Scientific Experiments for Young Children*; Seymour Simon, *How to be an Ocean Scientist in Your Own Home*; Robert Williams, Robert Rockwell, and Elizabeth Sherwood, *Mudpies to Magnets: A Preschool Science Curriculum*.

Using Nonfiction Picture Books

One of my main objectives with my students is to convey to them that science knowledge is a key factor in many narrative picture books and is just waiting to be capitalized upon. A second objective is to familiarize them with the wealth of nonfiction texts ideal for introducing, reinforcing, and illuminating science concepts. Beverly Kobrin in her book, *Eyeopeners! How to Choose and Use Children's Books About Real People, Places, and Things*, lists many wonderful nonfiction picture books that can be read aloud. In addition, she edits a newsletter that reviews many of the latest nonfiction books.

One important thing I have learned is that reading a nonfiction picture book aloud sometimes takes even more practice than a fiction book because the cadence is so different. In many nonfiction pieces, there is very little repetition. One concept follows another. The unsuspecting reader (who has not prepared the book ahead of time) can be caught sounding very disjointed (Myers, 1987).

For those who feel uncertain when trying to identify a science concept within a narrative text, it might be wise to take a transitional step somewhere between pure fiction and pure science. In fact, more and more picture books seem to be combining fiction and information genres. A wonderful example of this is seen in Joanna Cole's *The Magic School Bus at the Waterworks*. The book contains a definite fictional story line, but throughout we find such things as "water facts" and "notes from the author (for SERIOUS students only)" that provide teachers and students alike with the essence of the science concepts involved in the story.

Another wonderful example of combining genres is the book, *Where Fish Go in Winter: And Answers to Other Great Mysteries* by Amy Goldman Koss. This book of poems titles each poem with a question that any three- or four-year-old (or curious adult!) would be proud to ask: "What do clouds feel like?" The poem itself is then chock-full of actual scientific information to answer the question. This book as well as Joanna Cole's books could provide demonstrations to use with students for writing up what they have learned in science in any particular unit. It is also useful for them to realize that scientific information doesn't always have to be presented in a strict informational format.

A number of companies, however, are publishing series of informational picture books for children. One fine example is the A *New True Book* series by Children's Press of Chicago. One title in that series is *Experiments with Water* by Ray Broekel. This book can introduce students to important structures that differentiate fiction from nonfiction material. It has a table of contents, pictures with informational print attached, diagrams, actual experiments, and a glossary of terms. Having raised two children who have never lost their wonder about the world, I have come to realize that three- and four-year-olds can absorb a great deal about these informational structures when this kind of print makes a daily appearance in their lives. It is gratifying to observe in some first-grade classes where many informational books are constantly available and to see primary children comfortably using a table of contents or reading a graph in an adult book. As teachers at all levels move away from the concept of one textbook for the teaching of science, publishers are rushing to fill the void with many fine sets of informational books on topics that children of all ages are again coming to wonder about.

Conclusion

I hope that inservice as well as preservice teachers will come to again see themselves as scientists, as I have. One of the most important uses for picture books, both narrative and informational, would be to help teachers discover that curious, wondering child inside of themselves—the scientist—so they can support the scientist in each of their students.

Works Cited

Myers, Gary. March, 1987. "Reading Aloud for Information." *Teaching* K–8, 63.

Smith, Frank. 1985. *Reading Without Nonsense*. New York: Teacher's College.

Selected Bibliography For Science

Alexander, Alison and Susie Bower. 1986. *Science Magic: Scientific Experiments for Young Children*. New York: Prentice-Hall.

Bailes, Edith and Louis Lipovsky. 1984. *But Will It Bite Me?* Richmond, ME: Cardamom.

Broekel, Ray. 1988. *A New True Book: Experiments with Water*. Chicago: Children's Press.

Cole, Joanna. 1986. *The Magic School Bus at the Waterworks*. Illustrated by Bruce Degen. New York: Scholastic.

Kobrin, Beverly. 1988. *Eyeopeners! How to Choose and Use Children's Books About Real People, Places, and Things*. New York: Penguin.

Koss, Amy Goldman. 1987. *Where Fish Go in Winter and Answers to Other Great Mysteries*. Los Angeles: Price Stern Sloan.

McCloskey, Robert. 1957. *Time of Wonder*. New York: Viking.
Parnall, Peter. 1986. *Winter Barn*. New York: Macmillan.
Simon, Seymour. 1988. *How to Be an Ocean Scientist in Your Own Home*. Illustrated by David A. Carter. New York: Lippincott.
Smith, Kathie Billingslea. *Why?* Chicago: Rand McNally.
Williams, Robert, Robert Rockwell, and Elizabeth Sherwood (eds.). 1987. *Mudpies to Magnets: A Preschool Science Curriculum*. Mt. Rainier, MD: Gryphon House.
Zubrowski, Bernie. 1981. *Messing Around with Baking Chemistry*. Illustrated by Signe Hanson. Boston: Little, Brown.

11

Poetry and Picture Books: The Door to the Woods

Georgia Heard

I first remember picture books from when I was five. I gathered a handful of favorites and asked my mother to read them again and again. I can still see the pictures: Hansel's scared eyes, Gretel with her scarf tied around her head, both lost in the dark forest; Rapunzel's golden hair cascading down the tower wall, a vine for the witch to climb; and a strange German book called *Struvul Peter*, with Peter on the cover, his fingernails half a foot long.

My mother sat beside me on the bed; I stuck my thumb in my mouth and listened to her voice, musical as a flute and comforting as the steady sound of rain. I studied the pictures. I stared at them until I saw a door open into the book and I walked in. Then I was not just looking at Gretel walking helplessly through the woods, I *was* Gretel, stumbling over rocks after the bread crumbs disappeared. I was not just *reading* a book about Hansel and Gretel lost in the woods; my heart beat faster because I too was lost. This time of looking and listening was for me like the discovery the children made in C. S. Lewis's *The Lion, the Witch, and the Wardrobe*, when they accidentally open the back of their closet into a snowy woods. Each one of my favorite picture books opened the door from what I knew to many different worlds.

As a child I relied heavily on the pictures to pull me into the stories. The art invited me into the book immediately; I knew what kind of woods I was entering without having read a word. From the pictures alone I knew Rapunzel was locked in a tower and that the witch was evil and stood guard below, or that Hansel and Gretel were orphaned and had lost their way home. As I turned the pages, I could tell what was going to happen next. But when my mother read to me something else happened; the books took on an even deeper meaning. The words brought music to the silent world of art and became essential to the life of the book. Here is where the picture book's relationship to poetry is closest.

This same hypnotic pleasure of listening to the sounds of words, of stepping into another world, reoccurred years later when I first heard a poem. I don't remember the name of it, or its author, but it was about the silver scales of fish and the ripples of water in a pond. I was astonished at what it made me see. I wanted to hear it again, to hear the music of the words, to go back to that water where the fish swam. I was surprised that a poem could make me see and feel so much.

Poems rely on sounds as well as pictures to create a world. But in poetry the images embedded in the text are then painted in our minds. When I teach children to write poems, I suggest they try a technique I sometimes use when I write: try and see in their minds the image of their thoughts, feelings, and experiences. I tell them to gather the world around them—what they see, what they hear, taste, smell, and touch—and try and paint it, using words. The results of this journey are poems that are vivid and alive. Here is one by a third grader, Claire, who saw the image of the moon:

My Pet or Face in Moon

When I look at the moon in my car,
I think I just picked out a pet.
A pet that is mine and nobody elses.
My pet follows me around
where ever I go.

And Kara's poem about the dark:

The Dark

There was a switch in the sky
and an angel fly up and turned off the switch
and gave great dream and adventure
we thought were not possible.
And in the morning
an alarm clock woke the sun
and it started its work again.

We don't need to see a painting of the moon or the dark because Claire and Kara have painted the images so clearly using words.

My students ask what all writers ask: how, without actually drawing, can I use words to paint what is in my mind and heart? How can I make words seem real? Night seem like *night*? The moon last night? The feeling when my grandfather died?

Poets search for words that help the reader see the branches on the trees, the bark, even hear the bugs flying around them. We try and convey experience through images and through language that is concrete and visual, not abstract. I frequently suggest that my students stay away from abstract words like love or justice and instead use words that make a picture. For example, if I want to describe the spring, I wouldn't write simply "Spring is beautiful"; it's too vague. I might write, "Snow falls over the crocuses . . . " or something else that will help the reader see spring. The writer's task is not to pile on adjectives and descriptions but to select the exact words that will give us the experience he or she had. Rilke said, "for poems are not simply feelings, they are experiences." And it's through words that all writers convey experiences.

Picture books often have a similar richness and juxtaposition of word and picture. One good example is Cynthia Rylant's *Night in the Country*. The illustrations are beautiful blurry pastels of the night: a frog half-submerged in pond water, an owl with giant eyes ready to fly, an apple tree heavy with ripened fruit. Each page bears an image like the ones I might see when I close my eyes; but the whole story, the poetry of the night, doesn't really happen until I've read Rylant's words. It's in the words that I am able to experience the night as fully as Rylant experiences it: I hear the songs the frogs make as they sit in the pond, I see the owl's eyes as it takes off, I hear an apple fall on the ground. Through the images in the words, Rylant has opened the door to the night; I eagerly step inside.

One poetry tool that Rylant uses is metaphor and simile. When Rylant says the owl has "marble eyes", she is travelling to another world outside the owl's and transporting observations over here. Metaphor and simile make clear a relationship between two different images that were brought together in a union that is both surprising and pleasing. The eyes of an owl, and the inside of a marble.

Each writer must also lead us musically through the pages of words, like a conductor leading an orchestra. Poetry began as an oral art; like picture books, it is meant to be read aloud. Poems began as chants that invoked magic or told the story of a people and were handed down from generation to generation. The rhythm of words and lines was a way to help people sing and dance and remember the poems. We are bound to rhythm by the beat of our hearts, the passing of our breath, the cycles of days and seasons. When I hear a song on the radio my foot taps. Picture books share this musicality. Margaret Wise Brown uses song when in *Good Night Moon* she begins her litanies of good nights. She is singing. We hear the tune and want to sing with her. Many picture books share rhythms similar to those of poetry. Some of them, if written in poetic form, might be considered poetry. Many picture books use the same musical elements as poems do, like repetition and rhyme, to glue the story together. Sometimes picture books repeat a line over and over again throughout the book, as in Judith Viorst's funny *Alexander and the Horrible, No Good, Very Bad*

Day or in Cynthia Rylant's *The Relatives Came*. The first lines of a book sometimes repeat at the end, giving a circular feeling to the story, as in Riki Levinson's *Watch the Stars Come Out* or Donald Hall's *Ox-Cart Man*.

Both poets and picture book authors make musical compositions that depend on sound and silence. I had the pleasure of hearing Bijou Le Tord speak at my local library. After her talk, she passed around the manuscript of her book, *The Deep Blue Sea*. I expected to see loose paper; instead, her manuscript was on a story board. The board was covered with small squares filled with sketches; the words underneath looked like poems.

Bijou had divided the words into lines the way poets do. The end of a line and a stanza break in a poem are the musical equivalents of rests. Whenever there's white space in a poem, it signals a pause, even if for a very brief moment. Bijou and other picture book authors rely on this same relationship with silence. Poets create tension by enjambing some of their lines, stopping in mid-sentence to pull us to the next. Picture books also leave us suspended but at the end of a page; we have no choice but to turn. We read the word, then reach the silence, ford it, and the story begins again.

On one page of Rylant's *Night in the Country* is the single word "Listen": we wait to hear the sound of the apple falling in the night from the tree. We must turn the page to know what to listen for. On the next page is a pastel picture of an apple tree at night with one apple lying on the ground; at the bottom is the single word "Pump." To set a word off like that is to slow it down, to give it its own stage; it makes us rest there for a while. In this way, picture book authors alter the pace of their sentences, as poets do. They slow us down by putting only one word on a line, or speed up by crowding the page. The silence surrounding "pump" is also the silence of the night. One young student of mine, Jason, knew the power of slowing the reader down through line-breaks in his poem "Why?"

I just found out yesterday
that my grandfather died.
I really miss him.
He was a caring grandfather.
I really cared for him.
But he had to go.
Why
did
he
have
to
die?
Just
why?

Each single word on a line reflects the importance of Jason's question.

There is a stereotype that picture books are baby books, for people who can't read and need to look at pictures with few words. But I often use picture books with older students who are writing poems. Many picture books, if not actually poems, border on poetry and can certainly teach some of poetry's qualities.

Sometimes I ask students to choose a poem they love, one they've written or read, and turn it into a picture book. I suggest they study poems that have been turned into picture books like Robert Frost's *Birches* or *Stopping by Woods*, and then illustrate the central images of the poems they've chosen. In this process, the poem's images must be clear enough to illustrate; every word must be accurate and essential to the painting of the poem. Art then becomes a way of interpreting poems, and a way to help revise, making clear what doesn't belong.

A group of upper-grade students once chose to create their own picture book versions of Frost's *Stopping by Woods*. Each student had his own visual interpretation. One drew a man speaking the words as he led his horse through the woods; another painted a somber snow scene with an almost invisible horse walking through a dense forest; another painted a cheery man and a horse trotting through snowy woods. The students looked at the published version only after they had finished theirs, then gathered and compared the different books and discussed how they came to illustrate the poem their particular way.

Sometimes I suggest that my students go on a treasure hunt for the poetry hidden in picture books; they may find it in a musical passage, a metaphor, an image, or a beautiful line. A few combed through Jane Yolen's *Owl Moon* and found poetic lines; they then made a poem out of these lines, and learned to recognize the poetic in places other than in poetry books.

When I sit on the floor with older students and read them some of my favorite picture books, I try and read them as I would a poem—as one Native American said, "As if words in themselves have the power to make something happen." I watch their faces, quiet and open; and hope that perhaps for them too a door to the woods, to different worlds, has opened, and they're walking inside.

Works Cited

Lewis, C.S. 1986. *The Lion, the Witch, and the Wardrobe*. Illustrated by Pauline Baynes. New York: Macmillan.

Editor's Note:

In a recent New York Times *article, (4/15/90)* Bijou Le Tord *revealed much about the complex nature of her artistry as a writer and illustrator. Her books, which often appear to be deceptively simple, contain surprising messages for older readers and writers. The color-washed illustrations are intentionally uncluttered in order to "let the child's imagination imagine even more," but the sophisticated themes* Le Tord *chooses to focus upon are anything but simple. Beyond the intriguing subject matter,* Le Tord's *work offers valuable demonstrations about the importance of indepth research, the precise use of language and craft of distilling quintessential elements from a vast body of information. Her goal, she explains, is "to try to show and explain what I see and feel in a simple way." In the words that follow,* Le Tord *does just that.*

12

Research: An Adventure

Bijou Le Tord

Research is many things in my work: it is an adventure, a tool to help me be more authentic, a way to learn, a means of collecting and seeing things. Reading is the greatest part of this adventure. Everything I read and see is carefully recorded within me. This valuable information comes back to me at the precise moment I need it—when I create, when watercolor becomes sky, trees, a bird's feather. When words say what I want them to say, then I take from my collection of thoughts, emotions, and images.

Reading is one way for me to constantly add to my collection, to continue the adventure. I read more poetry than anything else because of the pictures in poems. I like to paint with words, as poets often do. Reading poetry makes me feel at peace with the world. It gives me warmth, like when you first meet someone you really like. At times it makes me feel like taking a pencil and immediately sitting down to work.

It happened that way when I read May Sarton's poem, "Seascape" (1984). In her poem there is a sentence that refers to the gentle singing of the sea. I had found a friend, someone who felt the same way I did. I thought, "She expresses a feeling I have and want to talk about." It moved me, and I too needed to talk about the sea, whales, birds in the air. But, I also wanted to say something about God creating all living creatures and the earth and its natural order. I had recently researched the Book of Genesis. Inspired by Sarton's poem and by my research, I found that words flew onto the page, and the story sparkled. May Sarton's sea was singing. My book, *The Deep Blue Sea*, was born.

At times I need a structure to build upon. While writing *Joseph and Nellie*, a book about a family of fishermen, it was important for me to know how to draw a real fishing boat. How big was it? Where, exactly, in the hull would the lower cabin be? Would the motor run on diesel fuel or gas? Was the vision I had of Joseph's and Nellie's life at sea a realistic one? Did it represent a typical life-style for a family, a husband and wife who worked side by side out on a trawler in the middle of the ocean? I had many questions, few answers.

Although I had spent a great deal of time on board many different kinds of boats, I needed reassurance. By chance, I have a friend who is a sea captain and naval architect. From his house on the Chesapeake Bay, we drew the plans for Joseph's and Nellie's new fishing trawler. We carefully designed every inch of their boat. It would be a forty-footer, big enough for our fishermen to make a good living. Small enough for two people to operate it safely and efficiently. I learned how to fold ropes neatly. I learned the meaning of starboard and portside lights while steering in and out of the harbor. It gave me the confidence I needed to go ahead and finish the illustrations with accuracy. From the beginning, my concern was whether Joseph's and Nellie's boat would float. And it did: it is still sailing across the sea.

Joseph and Nellie was authentic in every detail. I used the same diligence in designing the birdhouse for *Good Wood Bear*. Good Wood Bear makes houses to protect birds and their young. He works in his shed under the kind and watchful eye of his friend, Goose. Writing and illustrating *Good Wood Bear* required some knowledge of bird behavior, their seasonal patterns and feeding habits. To make sure the birdhouse plans (seen at the end of the book) were workable, I built two houses myself. I learned how to use a jigsaw and smoothing-plane, to choose the best wood I could find, to sand, and to paint. Being a bear-carpenter and a birdhouse-builder was fun. The birds were happy in their new homes.

Historical authenticity is equally important. *The Little Hills of Nazareth* gave me a chance to study the Bible. I enjoyed researching Jesus's homeland and finding out about the people of Israel as they lived two thousand years ago. Mary and Joseph became my friends. They took me along with Naboth, their little donkey, on a beautiful and fascinating journey.

If someone were to ask what makes research so important to the way I work, I would answer without hesitation, "Research adds dimension to my craft. It forces me to pay attention. It simplifies my work. It is probably the best tool a writer/artist has. There is no such thing as having too much information. Actually, one never has enough." Now, think of the adventure.

WORKS CITED

Sarton, May. 1984. *Letters from Maine: New Poems*. New York: Norton.

13

Illustrating Handel: A View from the Drawing Board

Ruth Tietjen Councell

When I first met with Patricia Gauch, editor in chief of Philomel Books, to discuss the possibility of illustrating a book about George Frederick Handel, I couldn't help catching her enthusiasm for the project. Author Bryna Stevens had written a lively and engaging tale based on events in the childhood of the composer. Pat was excited, first of all, about the chance to introduce young readers to the world of classical music. Secondly, she was excited about the prospect of making a fully illustrated picture book for older children, something not often done.

The project was attractive to me not only because of my interest in music, but also because it offered me an opportunity to attempt more challenging and involved illustrations. And I was reminded of my own experience in about the third grade of coming to the grim realization that, as I got older, books were getting thicker, type was getting smaller, and there were fewer and fewer pictures. Now, as an illustrator, I was delighted to be in a position to do something about what for me was a major childhood disappointment.

The challenges of illustrating *Handel and the Famous Sword Swallower of Halle* were the following:

1. To be faithful to the text in presenting a spirited young boy whose love of music prevails over opposition and obstacles.
2. To enhance the text by carefully researching costumes, settings, and customs of the period.

3. To make the book intriguing by adding humorous touches, secondary action, and visual clues to information not found in the text.

To be faithful to the text, an illustrator reads and rereads the story until it becomes so familiar that it is like looking at it from the inside out instead of the other way around. Images begin to bubble to the surface, ideas are jotted down, rough sketches are made, and eventually something vaguely cohesive begins to emerge. Just as in writing, an ongoing process of editing is necessary. Sometimes a good idea is eliminated in order to give balance or continuity to the whole.

An illustrator looks for key scenes, places of high energy or emotional impact. It is important to the flow of the book to space the scenes rhythmically. Once the scenes are chosen and laid out, the individual pictures can be developed.

To bring out young George's vitality, I gave his facial expressions and gestures lots of animation. I tried to convey his enthusiasm for music in as many scenes as possible. On one page he turns to listen to street musicians as he runs home from school. In another scene he claps his hands to the music of gypsies in the park. A shepherd playing to his sheep catches George's attention on his way to the castle. To convey young Handel's anguish at seeing his toy drum cast into the fire by his father, I emphasized the drama of the moment. The room is dark except for the raging fire in the center. The protesting figures of George and his aunt, arms upraised, are dramatically back-lit by the fire. In the shadows, his mother raises her hand to her mouth in alarm. A frightened kitten runs away. Toys are scattered. Facial expressions, gestures, lighting: all play a part in heightening the impact of the moment.

The research turned out to be the most challenging challenge of all and presented me with the most unexpected situations. Normally there are plenty of images to be found in costume books and paintings of a particular period. But after weeks of combing through libraries and coming up nearly empty handed, I was confused and frustrated. There were hundreds of pictures from the eighteenth century. But that was when George was an adult. There were plenty of costumes to be had from the first half of the seventeenth century, but that was before he was born. My little window in time was between 1685 and 1695. Even the curator of the costume collection at the Metropolitan Museum of Art in New York City was unable to help me. Finally the explanation to my dilemna was found in an art history book under the chapter heading, "Painting in Germany in the Late Seventeenth Century." It was a very short chapter that began by explaining that there was no painting in Germany in the late seventeenth century. I learned that the economy was in ruin from the Thirty Years War and the ravages of the plague. Most artists went to Italy or England in order to make a living.

I was beginning to identify with young Handel myself, trying to practice my art in the face of seemingly insurmountable obstacles. But gradually bits and pieces began to surface. A casual mention to friends at dinner brought out that they had in fact lived in Halle, the town of Handel's birth. They knew people there who were able to send me pictures of the town and brochures from the birthplace. A kind librarian allowed me access to some crumbling books of engravings, some of which were from the late seventeenth century. (Apparently engravers could still make a living.) An old German costume book turned up at the same library, and I was grateful for my elementary knowledge of the German language. A trip to the picture collection of the New York Public Library yielded some great and gory glimpses into medical practices of the day. (Handel's father was a barber/surgeon.) I would have xeroxed more had I not run out of dimes and been followed around by a questionable looking character. After two months of research I was finally ready to begin my work.

Though historical accuracy was important, it had to be kept in balance with the lively spirit of the story. This was not a biography but historical fiction. I used authentic references whenever possible, simplifying and stylizing places and people to create the overall feel. One scene gave me particular difficulty. I wanted to show how young George felt when he heard the sound of a great pipe organ. The text describes Handel, overwhelmed by the power of the booming organ, feeling the church might burst with the sound of the music. How could I depict a monstrously magnificent baroque organ and the expression on a little boy's face at the same time? After several attempts, I asked the advice of Dennis Nolan, an illustrator friend. He suggested making the horizon low to emphasize the organ's height and placing young George in the foreground fairly large and turning towards the organ just enough so we could still see his face. The perfect solution. Now all I needed was a picture of any impressive pipe organ built before 1690 as long as it was at the right angle for the composition. Back to the library. This time my search turned up a book of cathedrals printed in Germany in 1939 and last checked out in 1971. To my relief there appeared an interior showing a beautiful organ at just the right angle for my picture. But relief gave way to utter astonishment when I read the caption. It was Liebfrauens Kirche in Halle, the very church Handel had attended as a boy.

The third challenge, that of adding interest by means of background action, visual humor, and expanded bits of the story was as much fun as it was challenging. I enjoyed drawing the man sleeping in the church, the cat munching on a fish skeleton under the table, the mice in the attic. I had fun making the town gossips, the dog barking at the dancing bear, and the clergyman listening behind a pillar. And I hoped children would enjoy finding them. I also hoped they might find connections between some of the pictures and discover things about the story that were not told in the text. For example, one might notice George's mother holding a baby in one of the earlier scenes. Later on a small child and a second baby appear in the windows of the Handel house. And in the final scene, two little girls stand with their parents and wave good-bye to their big brother, George, as he goes off to study music. Though the author never mentions them, Handel did in fact have two younger sisters. Their presence in the book helps mark the passage of time and lend authenticity. But it can also lead one to look again and notice where they are as the book progresses.

To a person who has always enjoyed picture books, it seems only natural that there should be picture books for all ages. I look forward to the wonderful new directions this art form will take and to the enrichment it will bring to our children's lives and to ours. I for one will never outgrow my love for illustrated books and the magic, wisdom, beauty, and healing power they have within them.

14

Ann Turner: Reaching into the Past

Lenore Reilly Carlisle

Unlike so many of us who come to know and love history as adults or young adults, Ann Turner has always had an affinity for history. Growing up in New England, Ann was raised in a family that took its own history seriously. Indeed her ancestors, who came to America in the early seventeenth century, seem to have had a hand in just about every facet of American history. Whether presiding over colleges, hiding children in a trunk to escape from hostile neighbors during the Revolution, or chuckling about a note received from some eccentric poet in Amherst (none other than Emily Dickinson), the family somehow knew the importance of reaching into the past to make it part of the present.

But it was not the recounting of stories alone that drew Turner to history. In a recent interview, Ann spoke of her childhood memories, frequently mentioning objects that seemed to have piqued her interest in things historical. The trunk in the attic, her great grandmother's girlhood diary and letters to her dear cousin Adelaide, a tiny christening bonnet—this is the stuff of history that stimulated Turner's sense of romance about the past and that is clearly evident in so many of her books.

While Turner has sometimes turned to the novel as a place to explore her fascination with history, she has also had great success with the picture book genre. In contrast to the general assumption that picture books are intended for younger readers, many of Turner's picture books are more evocative to older readers. She is reflective about why certain stories seem to need to be told within the novel format, while others must come to life as picture books. As Turner sees it, her picture books tend to be about events more than they are about characters. Yes, *Nettie's Trip South* seems real to us because it presents a world peopled by individuals who feel so very deeply; but it is the trip itself, the journey during which slavery comes all too vividly to life for a young child, that is the dominant focus of Turner's vision. And again in *Dakota Dugout*, Turner is telling us not so much about what pioneering and homesteading were like for one woman, but rather offering us some universal truths about what it means to leave one's home behind and carve a new one out of an unfamiliar landscape.

In talking about this tendency to use the picture book to illuminate and elucidate a particular period in history, Turner calls forth language peppered with photographic imagery.

> I try to close in around a moment. It's as if there is this entire landscape, and I want just one circle of it. I want to focus on a particular moment during a particular time. It's like looking through a telescope. You know there is this enormous array of things before you, but your vision is bound by the rim. You get one real piece of it, one still shot.

Though Turner's books are comprised of several pages of both text and illustration, the reader has much the same feeling that comes from examining a single, poignant photograph from the Civil War. An entire history is embedded therein.

We sense this in *Nettie's Trip South*, a story of a child from the North who travels to the South before the Civil War and sees the cruelty of slavery. The world is seen through the eyes of eleven-year-old Nettie as she recounts her journey in a series of missives to her young cousin, Addie. Nettie is literally sickened by the inhumane treatment of enslaved Africans, and the trip changes her forever. As are so many of Turner's stories, *Nettie* is a story about losses and gains. Nettie's naivety and innocence are lost, but what she gains in her understanding of human suffering, injustice, and oppression is almost immeasurable.

Turner speaks with clarity about the recurring theme of loss and gain in her work. It is not surprising, she feels, that many of her books reflect that theme in some way since loss and gain so often pervade our sense of what a given historical moment in history is about. In *Heron Street*, a book that takes us through the industrialization of Boston, Turner poetically points out the losses one must endure if one is to experience certain gains. In fact, the original title of the book was *Bird Music—People Music*, reflecting Turner's belief that even in the midst of loss—loss of the purity of a time and place when the air was clean and quiet save for the songs of birds—there are gains: the gains of community and technology which create a music of their own.

Again in *Dakota Dugout* we see a woman who must endure the loss of her sense of what makes a home. And in the midst of that sense of loss, a new understanding of what can be gained from human struggle and endurance is born. In *Katie's Trunk*, to be published in the fall of 1992 by Macmillan, we encounter a character who experiences the devastating effects of political strife. Her sense of loss is enormous as the community she once understood to be unified and whole is torn apart by differing loyalties. Yet even here Turner tells us there are gains to be had as Katie comes to identify the threads of goodness that ultimately tie a community together.

That Turner should choose to write in a style that borders on the poetic is no surprise. As she speaks of how she chose to write certain books, there is a poetic yearning in her recollections: "*Dakota Dugout* was written because I had this image of a woman eating an apple in a dugout with sunlight streaming in on her as she gazed up through a paper window. That was the genesis of that book." Memories of family stories and artifacts stirred similar imagistic inspirations. From that initial inspiration, Turner's skill as a researcher, which matches her openness to the poetic muses, then comes into play.

Reflecting upon the use of picture books with older readers and writers, Turner sees the coming together of the two as being quite natural. Some of the moments she has captured and the stories she has to tell "simply couldn't come out any other way." That children are naturally given to an appreciation of the picture book is just a happy coincidence. Recognizing that history can sometimes seem overwhelming to children, Turner views picture books as a great way to "ease kids in through the back door." Her stories, she feels, are not overpowering. They have a clear beginning and a clear end. And while they may exist in some larger historical context, they have a valid and gripping life of their own.

At the same time she feels her stories are not overwhelming, Turner takes pride in her ability to tell children the truth about how difficult life can sometimes be. "I don't think it's good to deceive children about some of life's harsh realities. Seeing that the human spirit can prevail is important. I can remember so clearly reading about things the Ingalls' had to endure, especially in *The Long Winter* [Laura Ingalls Wilder]. And for me, that was an incredibly strength-giving book."

Turner's tremendous respect for children comes across when she speaks to them. To hear Turner talk to fourth and fifth graders about her books, and about how alive and lively history is for her personally, is to be let into something grand. She begins by giving students an opportunity to try their hand at historical research. Holding up a tiny christening bonnet and explaining that it was worn not by a doll but by a real baby, she asks children what conclusions they can come to about babies born around the time the bonnet was worn.

"Babies were smaller then!"

"Maybe the mothers were smaller too!"

When Turner asks why, the children eventually lite upon the role nutrition might have played. Another child begins to conjecture about how old babies might have been when the christening ceremony took place, and Turner is quick to get them guessing about how they could get that information. One child begins to imagine aloud the life of a particular baby and mother, and Turner enthusiastically interrupts:

> That's it! That's just what I do. I start to get interested in some object. It could be this or a snippet of a letter I've found. And as I study it and think about it, my imagination starts to play with the real things I know about the history of the time and a story begins to grow from that.

One can only hope that there are more attics to be explored in Ann Turner's life, more trunks to unpack, more baby bonnets to study. In reaching into the past, Turner has created jewels for the present.

WORKS CITED

Wilder, Laura Ingalls. 1940. *The Long Winter*. Illustrated by Garth Williams. New York: Harper & Row.

Bibliography of Picture Books

Ackerman, Karen. 1988. *Song and Dance Man*. Illustrated by Stephen Gammell. New York: Knopf.

Agee, Jon. 1988. *The Incredible Painting of Felix Clousseau*. New York: Farrar, Straus & Giroux.

Aliki. 1989. *The King's Day*. New York: Crowell.

———. 1983. *Fossils Tell of Long Ago*. New York: Harper & Row.

———. 1983. *A Medieval Feast*. New York: Harper Trophy.

———. 1979. *Mummies Made in Egypt*. New York: Harper Trophy.

———. 1979. *The Two of Them*. New York: Greenwillow.

Allard, Harry. 1989. *The Stupids Take Off*. Illustrated by James Marshall. Boston: Houghton Mifflin.

———. 1984. *The Stupids Have a Ball*. Illustrated by James Marshall. Boston: Houghton Mifflin.

———. 1981. *The Stupids Die*. Illustrated by James Marshall. Boston: Houghton Mifflin.

———. 1977. *The Stupids Step Out*. Illustrated by James Marshall. Boston: Houghton Mifflin.

Angelou, Maya. 1987. *Now Sheba Sings the Song*. Illustrated by Tom Feelings. New York: Dutton.

Anno, Mistumasa. 1989. *Anno's Aesop: A Book of Fable by Aesop and Mr. Fox*. New York: Orchard.

———. 1978. *Anno's Journey*. New York: Collins.

Baker, Olaf. 1981. *Where the Buffaloes Begin*. Illustrated by Stephen Gammell. New York: Puffin.

Bang, Molly Garrett. 1980. *The Grey Lady and the Strawberry Snatcher*. New York: Four Winds.

Base, Graeme. 1990. *My Grandma Lived in Gooligulch*. Davis, CA: The Australian Book Source.

———. 1988. *The Eleventh Hour*. New York: Viking Kestrel.

Baylor, Byrd. 1986. *I'm in Charge of Celebrations*. Illustrated by Peter Parnall. New York: Scribner's.

———. 1982. *Moon Song*. Illustrated by Ronald Himler. New York: Scribner's.

———. 1981. *Desert Voices*. Illustrated by Peter Parnall. New York: Scribner's.

———. 1980. *If You Are a Hunter of Fossils*. Illustrated by Peter Parnall. New York: Scribner's.

———. 1978. *The Other Way to Listen*. Illustrated by Peter Parnall. New York: Scribner's.

———. 1978. *The Way to Start a Day*. Illustrated by Peter Parnall. New York: Scribner's.

———. 1976. *Hawk, I Am Your Brother*. Illustrated by Peter Parnall. New York: Scribner's.

———. 1975. *The Desert Is Theirs*. Illustrated by Peter Parnall. New York: Aladdin.

———. 1974. *Everybody Needs a Rock*. Illustrated by Peter Parnall. New York: Scribner's.

Bemelmans, Ludwig. 1977. *Madeline*. New York: Penguin.

Birdseye, Tom. 1988. *Airmail to the Moon*. Illustrated by Stephen Gammell. New York: Holiday House.

Blos, Joan. 1987. *Old Henry*. Illustrated by Stephen Gammell. New York: Morrow.

Brady, Irene. 1976. *Wild Mouse*. New York: Scribner's.

Brett, Jan. 1990. *The Wild Christmas Reindeer*. New York: Putnam's.

———. 1989. *Beauty and the Beast*. New York: Clarion.

———. 1989. *The Mitten*. New York: Putnam's.

———. 1988. *The First Dog*. San Diego, CA: Harcourt Brace Jovanovich.

———. 1987. *Goldilocks and the Three Bears*. New York: Dodd, Mead.

———. 1985. *Annie and the Wild Animals*. Boston: Houghton Mifflin.

———. 1981. *Fritz and the Beautiful Horses*. Boston: Houghton Mifflin.

Brimner, Larry Dane. 1991. *Country Bear's Surprise*. Illustrated by Ruth Tietjen Councell. New York: Orchard.

———. 1988. *Country Bear's Good Neighbor*. Illustrated by Ruth Tietjen Councell. New York: Orchard.

Brown, Marc. 1985. *Arthur's Tooth*. Boston: Little, Brown.

Brown, Margaret Wise. 1947. *Good Night Moon*. Illustrated by Clement Hurd. New York: Harper & Row.

Browne, Anthony. 1986. *Piggybook*. New York: Knopf.

Buck, Margaret. 1964. *Along the Seashore*. New York: Abingdon.

Bunting, Eve. 1991. *Fly Away Home*. Illustrated by Ronald Himler. New York: Clarion.

Burkert, Nancy Ekholm. 1989. *Valentine & Orson*. New York: Farrar, Straus & Giroux.

Burningham, John. 1986. *Where's Julius?* New York: Crown.

———. 1977. *Come Away From the Water, Shirley*. New York: Crowell.

Burton, Virginia. 1939. *Mike Mulligan and His Steam Shovel*. Boston: Houghton Mifflin.

Carroll, Lewis. 1989. *Jabberwocky*. Retold and illustrated by Graeme Base. New York: Abrams.

Cendrars, Blaise. 1982. *Shadow*. Translated from the French & illustrated by Marcia Brown. New York: Scribner's.

Chaucer, Geoffrey. 1988. *Canterbury Tales*. Selected, translated, and adapted by Barbara Cohen. Illustrated by Trina Schart Hyman. New York: Lothrop, Lee & Shepard.

Cherry, Lynne. 1990. *The Great Kapok Tree*. New York: Harcourt Brace Jovanovich.

Cole, Joanna. 1990. *The Magic School Bus Lost in the Solar System*. Illustrated by Bruce Degen. New York: Scholastic.

———. 1988. *The Magic School Bus Inside the Human Body*. Illustrated by Bruce Degen. New York: Scholastic.

———. 1986. *The Magic School Bus Inside the Earth*. Illustrated by Bruce Degen. New York: Scholastic.

———. 1986. *The Magic School Bus at the Waterworks*. Illustrated by Bruce Degen. New York: Scholastic.

———. 1981. A *Horse's Body*. Photographs by Jerome Wexler. New York: Morrow.

Collington, Peter. 1987. *The Angel and the Soldier Boy*. New York: Knopf.

Cooney, Barbara. 1990. *Hattie and the Wild Waves*. New York: Viking.

———. 1988. *Island Boy*. New York: Viking Kestrel.

———. 1982. Miss *Rumphius*. New York: Viking Kestrel.

d'Aulaire, Ingri and Edgar. 1952. *Buffalo Bill*. Garden City, NJ: Doubleday.

DeBrunhoff, Laurent. 1987. *Babar Comes to America*. New York: Random House.

De Gerez, Toni Louni. 1986. *Witch of North Farm*. Illustrated by Barbara Cooney. New York: Viking Kestrel.

dePaola, Tomie. 1983. *The Legend of the Blue Bonnet*. New York: Putnam's.

———. 1981. *The Hunter and the Animal*. New York: Holiday House.

———. 1981. *Now One Foot, Now the Other*. New York: Putnam.

———. 1979. *The Kids' Cat Book*. New York: Holiday House.

———. 1973. *Nana Upstairs and Nana Downstairs*. New York: Putnam.

Disney Publications. 1972. *Walt Disney's Three Little Pigs*. New York: Random House.

Emberly, Michael. 1990. *Ruby*. Boston: Little, Brown.

Farber, Norma. 1979. *How Does It Feel to Be Old?* Illustrated by Trina Schart Hyman. New York: Dutton.

Feelings, Muriel. 1974. *Jambo Means Hello*. Illustrated by Tom Feelings. New York: Dial.

Fisher, Leonard Everett. 1987. *The Tower of London*. New York: Macmillan.

———. 1986. *The Great Wall of China*. New York: Macmillan.

Fleischman, Paul. 1988. *Rondo in C*. Illustrated by Janet Wentworth. New York: Harper & Row.

Fonteyn, Margot. 1989. *Swan Lake*. Illustrated by Trina Schart Hyman. San Diego, CA: Gulliver.

Fox, Mem. 1985. *Wilfred Gordon MacDonald Partridge*. Illustrated by Julie Vivas. New York: Kane/Miller.

———. 1983. *Possum Magic*. Illustrated by Julie Vivas. Nashville, TN: Abingdon.

Frost, Robert. 1988. *Birches*. Illustrated by Ed Young. New York: Holt.

———. 1978. *Stopping by Woods on a Snowy Evening*. Illustrated by Susan Jeffers. New York: Dutton.

Gag, Wanda. 1928. *Millions of Cats*. New York: Coward-McCann.

Garelick, May. 1973. *Down to the Beach*. Illustrated by Barbara Cooney. New York: Four Winds.

Goble, Paul. 1989. *Beyond the Ridge*. New York: Bradbury.

———. 1987. *Death of the Iron Horse*. New York: Bradbury.

———. 1984. *Buffalo Woman*. New York: Bradbury.

Godden, Rumer. 1985. *The Story of Holly and Ivy*. Illustrated by Barbara Cooney. New York: Viking Kestrel.

Goffstein, M.B. 1976. *Fish for Supper*. New York: Dial.

Goodall, John S. 1986. *The Story of a Castle*. New York: Macmillan.

Grahame, Kenneth. 1977. *The River Bank*. Illustrated by Adrienne Adams. New York: Scribner's.

Greenfield, Eloise. 1981. *Daydreamers*. Illustrated by Tom Feelings. New York: Dial.

Grimes, Nikki. 1986. *Something on My Mind*. Illustrated by Tom Feelings. New York: Dial.

Grimm, Jacob and Wilhelm K. 1989. *Dear Mili: An Old Tale*. Translated by R. Maneim and Illustrated by Maurice Sendak. New York: Michael de Capua.

Guarino, Deborah. 1989. *Is Your Mama a Llama?* Illustrated by Steven Kellogg. New York: Scholastic.

Hall, Donald. 1984. *The Man Who Lived Alone*. Illustrated by Mary Azarian. Boston: Godine.

———. 1979. *The Ox-Cart Man*. Illustrated by Barbara Cooney. New York: Viking Kestrel.

Hamanaka, Sheila. *The Journey: Japanese Americans, Racism, and Renewal*. New York: Orchard.

Haseley, Dennis. 1986. *Kite Flier*. Illustrated by David Weisner. New York: Four Winds.

Heller, Ruth. 1988. *Kites Sail High*. New York: Grossett and Dunlap.

Helprin, Mark. 1989. *Swan Lake*. Illustrated by Chris Van Allsburg. Boston: Ariel.

Hoban, Russell. 1974. *How Tom Beat Captain Najork and His Hired Sportsmen*. Illustrated by Quentin Blake. New York: Atheneum.

Hodges, Margaret. 1984. *St. George and the Dragon*. Illustrated by Trina Schart Hyman. Boston: Little, Brown.

Holling, Holling C. 1941. *Paddle-to-the-Sea*. Boston: Houghton Mifflin.

Hutchins, Pat. 1968. *Rosie's Walk*. New York: Macmillan.

Hyman, Trina S. 1983. *Little Red Riding Hood*. New York: Holiday House.

———. 1979. *The Sleeping Beauty*. Boston: Little, Brown.

———. 1974. *Snow White*. Translated by Paul Heins. Boston: Little, Brown.

Innocenti, Roberto. 1985. *Rose Blanche*. Mankato, MN: Creative Education.

Johnston, Tony. 1985. *The Quilt Story*. Illustrated by Tomie dePaola. New York: Putnam's.

Keats, Ezra Jack. 1987. *The Trip*. New York: Morrow.

Kellogg, Steven. 1988. *Johnny Appleseed*. New York: Morrow.

———. 1986. *Best Friends*. New York: Dutton.

———. 1986. *Pecos Bill*. New York: Morrow.

———. 1973. *The Island of the Skog*. New York: Dial.

Kesselman, Wendy. 1980. *Emma*. Illustrated by Barbara Cooney. New York: Doubleday.

Krauss, Ruth. 1945. *The Carrot Seed*. Illustrated by Crockett Johnson. New York: Harper & Row.

LaFontaine, Jean de. 1963. *The Lion and the Rat*. Illustrated by Brian Wildsmith. New York: Watts.

Lasky, Kathryn, 1988. *Sea Swan*. Illustrated by Catherine Stock. New York: Macmillan.

———. 1963. *Sugaring Time*. Photographs by Christopher G. Knight. New York: Macmillan Aladdin.

Le Tord, Bijou. 1991. *The Little Sheperd: The Twenty-Third Psalm*. New York: Delacorte.

———. 1990. *The Deep Blue Sea*. New York: Orchard.
———. 1988. *Little Hills of Nazareth*. New York: Bradbury.
———. 1986. *Joseph and Nellie*. New York: Bradbury.
———. 1985. *Good Wood Bear*. New York: Bradbury.
Levison, Riki. 1985. *Watch the Stars Come Out*. Illustrated by Diane Goode. New York: Dutton.
Lewis, Richard. 1991. *All of You Was Singing*. Illustrated by Ed Young. New York: Atheneum.
Lionni, Leo. 1967. *Frederick*. New York: Knopf.
Lobel, Arnold. 1972. *Frog and Toad Together*. New York: Harper & Row.
Locker, Thomas. 1984. *Where the River Begins*. New York: Dial.
Longfellow, Henry Wadsworth. 1983. *Hiawatha*. Illustrated by Susan Jeffers. New York: Dial.
Lyon, George Ella. 1990. *Come a Tide*. Illustrated by Stephen Gammell. New York: Orchard.

Maestro, Betsy. 1986. *The Story of the Statue of Liberty*. Illustrated by Guilio Maestro. New York: Lothrop, Lee, & Shepard.
Macaulay, David. 1990. *Black and White*. Boston: Houghton Mifflin.
———. 1988. *The Way Things Work*. Boston: Houghton Mifflin.
———. 1977. *Castle*. Boston: Houghton Mifflin.
———. 1975. *Pyramid*. Boston: Houghton Mifflin.
———. 1973. *Cathedral*. Boston: Houghton Mifflin.
McCloskey, Robert. 1957. *Time of Wonder*. New York: Viking.
McKissack, Patricia C. 1988. *Mirandy and Brother Wind*. Illustrated by Jerry Pinkney. New York: Knopf.
McMillan, Bruce. 1977. *Finestkind O'Day*. Philadelphia, PA: Lippincott.
Malotki, Ekkehart (reteller). 1988. *The Mouse Couple*. Illustrated by Michael Lacapa. Flagstaff, AZ: Northland.
Marshall, James. 1988. *Goldilocks and the Three Bears*. New York: Dial.
———. 1987. *Red Riding Hood*. New York: Dial.
Martin Jr., Bill and John Archambault. 1987. *Knots on a Counting Rope*. Illustrated by Ted Rand. New York: Holt.
———. 1986. *Barn Dance!* Illustrated by Ted Rand. New York: Holt.
———. 1985. *The Ghost-Eve Tree*. Illustrated by Ted Rand. New York: Holt, Rinehart and Winston.
Mayer, Mercer. 1986. *There's a Nightmare in My Closet*. New York: Dial.
Miles, Miska. 1971. *Annie and the Old One*. Illustrated by Peter Parnall. Boston: Little, Brown.
Murphy, Jim. 1988. *The Last Dinosaur*. Illustrated by Mark Alan Weatherby. New York: Scholastic.
Musgrove, Margaret. 1976. *Ashanti to Zulu: African Traditions*. Illustrated by Leo and Diane Dillon. New York: Dial.

Olson, Arielle. 1987. *The Lighthouse Keeper's Daughter*. Illustrated by Elaine Wentworth. Boston: Little, Brown.
Ormerod, Jan. 1981. *Sunshine*. New York: Viking Penguin.

Parnall, Peter. 1990. *Woodpile*. New York: Macmillan.
———. 1989. *Cats from Away*. New York: Macmillan.
———. 1989. *Quiet*. New York: Morrow.
———. 1988. *Apple Tree*. New York: Macmillan.
———. 1988. *Feet*. New York: Macmillan.
———. 1986. *Winter Barn*. New York: Macmillan.
———. 1984. *The Day Watchers*. New York: Macmillan.
———. 1975. *Alfalfa Hill*. New York: Doubleday.
Peet, Bill. 1970. *The Whingdingdilly*. Boston: Houghton Mifflin.
———. 1970. *The Wump World*. Boston: Houghton Mifflin.
Pittman, Helene Clare. 1988. *Once When I Was Scared*. Illustrated by Ted Rand. New York: Dutton.
Prelutsky, Jack. 1982. *The Baby Uggs Are Hatching*. Illustrated by Stevenson. New York: Greenwillow.

Rey, H. A. 1941. *Curious George*. Boston: Houghton Mifflin.
Ringgold, Faith. 1991. *Tar Beach*. New York: Crown.
Robbins, Ken. 1990. *A Flower Grows*. New York: Dial.
Rylant, Cynthia. 1988. *All I See*. Illustrated by Peter Catalanotto. New York: Orchard.
———. 1986. *Night in the Country*. Illustrated by Mary Szilagyi. New York: Bradbury.
———. 1985. *The Relatives Came*. Illustrated by Stephen Gammell. New York: Bradbury.
———. 1984. *Waiting to Waltz–A Childhood*. Illustrated by Stephen Gammell. New York: Bradbury.
———. 1982. *When I Was Young in the Mountains*. Illustrated by Diane Goode. New York: Dutton.

Sandburg, Carl. 1950. *The Wedding Procession of the Rag Doll and the Broom Handle and Who Was in It*. Illustrated by Harriet Pincus. New York: Harcourt Brace Jovanovich.
Schonberg, Virginia. 1969. *The Salt Marsh*. New York: Morrow.
Schwartz, Amy. 1988. *Annabelle Swift, Kindergartener*. New York: Orchard.
Sendak, Maurice. 1981. *Outside Over There*. New York: Harper & Row.
———. 1970. *In the Night Kitchen*. New York: Harper & Row.
———. 1963. *Where the Wild Things Are*. New York: Harper & Row.
———. 1962. *Alligators All Around*. New York: Harper & Row.
———. 1962. *Chicken Soup with Rice*. New York: Harper & Row.
———. 1962. *One Was Johnny*. New York: Harper & Row.

———. 1962. *Pierre.* New York: Harper & Row.

Service, Robert. 1986. *The Cremation of Sam McGee.* Illustrated by Ted Harrison. New York: Greenwillow.

Seuss, Dr. (A. S. Geisel). 1986. *You're Only Old Once!* New York: Random House.

———. 1984. *The Butter Battle Book.* New York: Random House.

———. 1956. *If I Ran the Circus.* New York, Random House.

Shor, Pekay. 1973. *When the Corn is Red.* Illustrated by Gary Von Ilg. New York: Abingdon.

Shulevitz, Uri. 1978. *The Treasure.* New York: Farrar, Straus & Giroux.

Siebert, Diane. 1989. *Heartland.* Illustrated by Wendell Minor. New York: Crowell.

———. 1988. *Mojave.* Illustrated by Wendel Minor. New York: Crowell.

Silverstein, Shel. 1974. *Where the Sidewalk Ends.* New York: Harper & Row.

———. 1964. *The Giving Tree.* New York: Harper & Row.

Simon, Seymour. 1988. *How To be An Ocean Scientist in Your Own Home.* Illustrated by David A. Carter. New York: Lippencott.

Sneve, Virginia Driving Hawk. 1989. *Dancing Teepees.* Illustrated by Stephen Gammell. New York: Holiday House.

Spier, Peter. 1980. *People.* Garden City, NJ: Doubleday.

Stanley, Diane. 1986. *Peter the Great.* New York: Four Winds.

Stanley, Diane, and Peter Vennema. 1988. *Shaka, King of the Zulus.* Illustrated by Diane Stanley. New York: Morrow.

Stanley, Fay. 1991. *The Last Princess: The Story of Princess Ka'iulani of Hawai'i.* Illustrated by Diane Stanley. New York: Four Winds.

Steig, William. 1980. *Gorky Rises.* New York: Farrar, Straus & Giroux.

———. 1971. *Amos and Boris.* New York: Farrar, Straus & Giroux.

Steptoe, John (reteller). 1984. *The Story of Jumping Mouse.* New York: Lothrop, Lee & Shepard.

Stevens, Bryna. 1990. *Handel and the Famous Sword Swallower of Halle.* Illustrated by Ruth Tietjen Councell. New York: Philomel Books.

Symes, R.F. and the staff of the Natural History Museum, London. 1988. *Rocks and Minerals.* With photographs; Neville Graham, art editor. New York: Knopf.

Tashlin, Frank. 1946. *The Bear That Wasn't.* New York: Dover.

Thaler, Mike. 1989. *The Teacher From the Black Lagoon.* Illustrated by Jared Lee. New York: Scholastic.

Thayer, Ernest. 1978. *Casey at the Bat.* Illustrated by Wallace Tripp. New York: Coward, McCann & Geoghegan.

Tunis, Edwin. 1957. *Colonial Living.* New York: World.

Turner, Ann. In press. *Katie's Trunk.* New York: Macmillan.

———. 1989. *Heron Street.* Illustrated by Lisa Desimini. New York: Harper & Row.

———. 1987. *Nettie's Trip South*. Illustrated by Ronald Himler. New York: Macmillan.
———. 1985. *Dakota Dugout*. Illustrated by Ronald Himler. New York: Macmillan.

Udry, Janice. 1956. *A Tree is Nice*. Illustrated by Marc Simont. New York: Harper & Row.
Ungerer, Tomi. 1970. *The Hat*. New York: Parents Magazine.

VanAllsburg, Chris. 1990. *Just a Dream*. Boston: Houghton Mifflin.
———. 1988. *Two Bad Ants*. Boston: Houghton Mifflin.
———. 1985. *The Polar Express*. Boston: Houghton Mifflin.
———. 1983. *The Wreck of the Zephyr*. Boston: Houghton Mifflin.
———. 1981. *Jumanji*. Boston: Houghton Mifflin.
Viorst, Judith. 1972. *Alexander and the Horrible, No Good, Very Bad Day*. Illustrated by Ray Cruz. New York: Atheneum.
———. 1969. *I'll Fix Anthony*. Illustrated by Arnold Lobel. New York: Harper & Row.
Vivas, Julie. 1986. *The Nativity*. San Diego, CA: Gulliver.

Walker, Alice. 1988. *To Hell with Dying*. Illustrated by Catherine Deeter. San Diego, CA: Harcourt Brace Jovanovich.
Weisner, David. 1988. *Free Fall*. New York: Lothrop, Lee & Shepard.
Wheatley, Nadia and Donna Rawlins. 1987. *My Place*. Melbourne, Australia: Collins Dove.
Wild, Margaret. 1989. *The Very Best of Friends*. Illustrated by Julie Vivas. New York: Harcourt Brace Jovanovich.
Willard, Nancy. 1987. *The Mountains of Quilt*. Illustrated by Tomie dePaola. San Diego, CA: Harcourt Brace Jovanovich.
———. 1983. *Nightgown of the Sullen Moon*. Illustrated by David McPhail. New York: Harcourt Brace Jovanovich.
Williams, Vera B. 1988. *String Bean's Trip to the Shining Sea*. New York: Greenwillow.
———. 1982. *A Chair for My Mother*. New York: Scholastic.
Willis, Val. 1988. *The Secret in the Matchbox*. Illustrated by John Shelley. New York: Farrar, Straus & Giroux.
Wittman, Sally. 1969. *A Special Trade*. Illustrated by Karen Gundersheimer. New York: Harper & Row.
Wood, Audrey. 1987. *Heckedy Peg*. Illustrated by Don Wood. San Diego, CA: Harcourt Brace Jovanovich.
———. 1985. *King Bidgood's in the Bathtub*. Illustrated by Don Wood. San Diego, CA: Harcourt Brace Jovanovich.
———. 1985. *The Napping House*. Illustrated by Don Wood. San Diego, CA: Harcourt Brace Jovanovich.

———. 1980. *Moon Flute*. Illustrated by Don Wood. San Diego, CA: Harcourt Brace Jovanovich.

Wright, Joan. 1987. *Bugs*. Illustrated by Nancy Winslow Parker. New York: Greenwillow.

Yolen, Jane. 1987. *Owl Moon*. Illustrated by John Schoenherr. New York: Putnam.

———. 1981. *Sleeping Ugly*. Illustrated by Diane Stanley. New York: Putnam.

Young, Ed. 1989. *Lon Po Po: A Red-Riding Hood Story from China*. New York: Philomel.

Zolotow, Charlotte. 1984. *I Know a Lady*. Illustrated by James Stevenson. New York: Penguin.

———. 1977. *Mr. Rabbit and the Lovely Present*. Illustrated by Maurice Sendak. New York: Harper & Row.

9368